PSALMS
for the
JOURNEY

PSALMS
for the
JOURNEY

THE LORD'S SONG IN ORDINARY TIME

LARRY R. KALAJAINEN

UPPER
ROOM BOOKS
NASHVILLE

Cover design: Jim Bateman
Cover photograph: SuperStock, Inc.
Interior design and layout: Nancy Cole
First Printing: June 1996 (7)

LIBRARY OF CONGRESS CATALOGING-IN-PUBLICATION DATA

KALAJAINEN, LARRY R.
    Psalms for the journey: the Lord's song in ordinary time / by Larry R. Kalajainen
    p.   cm.
    Includes bibliographical references.
    ISBN: 0-8358-0780-0
    1. Bible. O.T. Psalms—Study and teaching. 2. Bible. O.T. Psalms—Meditations. I. Title.
BS1430.5.K35   1996
223' .2'007—dc20   96-12402
                                                                      CIP

Printed in the United States of America

I lovingly dedicate this book to my mother and father,

Dorothy and Robert Kalajainen,

who first taught me to love the scriptures

and who encouraged my first steps on the journey of faith

Contents

Introduction

For nearly three millennia, a collection of 150 Hebrew poems, prayers, hymns, and liturgical pieces has served as the most important prayer book of the Jewish and Christian religious communities. Whether chanted by a cantor in the synagogue or by medieval monks in choir, whether recomposed as hymns by Protestant Reformers or used as reading primers by the early American settlers in Massachusetts, the Book of Psalms holds an unparalleled place of honor in the culture and spirituality of both Judaism and Christianity. While still a part of some denominational traditions, psalm-singing as a vital part of worship died out in others. But the use of the psalms in worship as responsive readings and in private prayer remained alive.

Some revisions of denominational hymnals have reintroduced psalm-singing and psalm-chanting in an attempt to rekindle the ancient connection between the psalms and music. Composers of anthems have always found abundant material for their compositions in the psalms. The title of the collection itself connects the psalms with singing. The English title Psalms is a transliteration of the Greek *psalmoi*, which means "songs of praise." This title first appears in Greek translations of the Old Testament; the oldest Hebrew manuscripts do not have a title. Various collections of Jewish rabbinical literature describe the psalms as prayers, book of praises, or simply praise.[1]

Of course, the earliest Christians were Jews. The scriptures that nourished them also nourished the Galilean teacher and prophet Jesus of Nazareth, in whose life they had come to believe God had been present in a unique way. As they reread those scriptures—particularly the psalms and the writings of the Hebrew prophets—in light of their experience of Jesus' life and death, they received the interpretive keys to understanding the meaning of those events as well as the significance of Jesus himself.

The New Testament quotes the psalms, along with the prophetic writings we know as The Book of Isaiah, more than any other part of the Hebrew Scriptures. Psalms 22, 31, and 69 often are called the Passion psalms, since they are deeply woven into the very fabric of the Gospel narratives of Jesus' passion. Many, if not most, of the Christological titles by which the New Testament names and interprets Jesus come from the psalms.

WHY WERE THE PSALMS REGARDED SO HIGHLY in both Judaism and Christianity? Why did the earliest Christians look to the psalms to figure out the meaning of the events surrounding Jesus of Nazareth? Perhaps the view of Athanasius, the fourth-century bishop of Alexandria, says it best:

> It is my view that in the words of this book [the Book of Psalms] the whole human life, its basic spiritual conduct and as well its occasional movements and thoughts is comprehended and contained. *Nothing to be found in human life is omitted* (emphasis mine).[2]

The abiding appeal of the psalms is precisely the accurate and comprehensive way in which they give voice to all the diverse experiences of human life in the context of prayer. From the most euphoric moments of celebration, joy, and happiness to the most crushing moments of depression, helplessness, and anger, the psalms speak for all of us. Not only do they speak; they speak eloquently. The form of Hebrew poetry, with its characteristic parallel repetitions, provides an elegant vehicle for the expression of the heights and the depths of human experience. Generations of Christians have taken comfort from the majestic cadences of Psalm 23 or Psalm 90 at the burial and memorial services of their loved ones. I well remember from my childhood days the tradition of always reading Psalm 121 when family members were preparing to leave on long journeys. From life's most mundane occasions to the most exalted, the psalms provide a language to give voice to our feelings and thoughts.

BUT THE CONTINUING APPEAL OF THE PSALMS is not only that they help us articulate the full range of our experiences and emotions; they offer us that help in the context of prayer. The psalms are primarily human speech to God. They arose out of the life of a praying community, Israel, responding to its experiences in the context of relationship to God. Many great works of literature voice the human situation eloquently; few of them voice it in the form of prayer. The psalms speak for us as human beings, and more particularly, as praying beings. It is not merely life itself, but life lived in relationship to, and in conversation with, God that permeates the psalms. As in any intimate relationship, the conversation is by turns, happy, thankful, loving, complaining, nagging, and angry. The speakers in the psalms are at various times honest, hypocritical, self-righteous, vengeful, humble, and penitent, as we are. All of them reveal their inner selves in prayer.

This is precisely why Jews and Christians have placed such importance on the psalms. Human beings, ourselves among them, do not naturally reveal our true inner selves in prayer. Frequently our prayers are vehicles for presenting ourselves to God in the best possible light or for approaching God in a manner calculated to gain God's favorable attention. We find it hard to allow God to see our true feelings and motives.

For instance, who among us would feel comfortable allowing God to know that we were capable of such vengeful hatred that we would wish to hurl our enemy's children against the rocks (Psalm 137:9)? Yet deep down inside, we know we are capable of feeling that angry and vengeful. And we know that such vengefulness plays itself out all too frequently in families and in nations. As of this writing, such horrific, unspeakably barbaric and fratricidal acts are an everyday occurrence in Bosnia and Rwanda. The depths of disaffection and rage displayed in the bombing of the federal building in Oklahoma City shocked Americans, and sophisticated Parisians are learning to cope with terrorist bombings in metro stations and tourist sites.

Would it not be far safer to voice those inner rages, lusts, and hatreds to God, so that in God's presence, we could discover healing? That is why we need the psalms. They teach us how to uncover our true selves to God, so that God's word and saving love can transform our inner selves and disarm the savage emotions that we harbor there.

THIS BOOK ATTEMPTS TO MAKE THE PSALMS more accessible to those who wish to use them as a resource for prayer and spiritual growth. The canonical order of the psalms does not necessarily follow the experiential order of life. The Book of Psalms itself is subdivided into five books, probably to correspond to the five books of the Torah (the first five books of the Hebrew Scriptures, or Old Testament). Each of the five books includes the differing types of psalms—but in various, and sometimes random, combinations.

I have chosen to structure these exercises according to six common experiences or movements of human life that find voice in the psalms. I have characterized each of the six movements (and there are undoubtedly more than these I've identified) by one word, either an adverb or a preposition. Why adverbs and prepositions? Because they are words that imply motion. The words are *up, down, through, during, from,* and *upon.* The human experiences in relationship to God that correspond to each of these motions respectively are *praise and presence, absence, struggle and growth, waiting, deliverance,* and *confidence and trust.* Most of us will be experiencing more than one of these motions simultaneously. Human development and spiritual maturation is never a straight-line affair. If our life is a life lived in relationship to God and others, then there is dynamic movement and change. A static relationship is no relationship at all. Engagement and encounter belong to the essence of relationships—stops and starts, wrong turnings, dead ends, new beginnings, dangerous curves, and smooth straightaways.

I have chosen five psalms that give voice to these movements of the soul for each of the six movements. I decided to work on the principle of a five-day week, assuming that many will find their weekends so fully scheduled that an exercise for Saturdays and Sundays might become burdensome.

One note of caution: Each day's exercise may contain more material than any one person can cope with in the time one has to spend on it. *Do not feel obligated to answer every question or engage every issue every day.* Some days you may want to spend your whole time on one of the reflection questions; other days, you will have time for two or more. I would suggest reading over all the reflection questions under LEARNING THE MUSIC each day. Then focus on the one or two that you find most intriguing or disquieting. Use the book according to *your* needs.

THIS STUDY IS DESIGNED for use by individuals as a resource for deepening one's personal prayer. However, since all personal prayer is rooted in the prayer of the faith community, I have included a group session at the close of each week to facilitate the use of the book by small groups within congregations. Many have found the individual work combined with a group in which to share insights and questions an effective means of personal growth.

Unlike the two previous books in this series *A Lenten Journey: Travels in the Spiritual Life Based on the Gospel According to Mark* and *An Advent Journey: Preparing the Way of the Lord* (both published by Upper Room Books), this study does not center around one of the major festivals on the church calendar. It is designed expressly for use during the substantial stretches of the year between the great feast days, that time referred to liturgically as Ordinary Time. Ordinary Time is not dull, routine, or boring time. Ordinary time is not time when nothing important is happening. Rather, Ordinary Time is the time of our lives, hallowed by the saving acts of God in Jesus Christ and celebrated at the great festivals. Ordinary Time is human time; it is time in which we are to live out the gospel story in the round of ordinary life.

Since both Jews and Christians alike traditionally have sung the psalms, the theme of singing seemed a natural metaphor for the movements of the spiritual life in Ordinary Time. The structure of each day's exercise carries this theme through the musical terminology. I encourage the use of a hymnal along with the book. Then if the hymnal contains settings of some of the psalms in the study, you may choose to sing the Lord's song literally as well as figuratively. You also may want to read an article on the Psalms in a Bible dictionary such as the one-volume *Harper's Bible Dictionary* to gain more information on the various literary forms and types of psalms and the occasions that may have given rise to them. The *Anchor Bible Dictionary* and the older *Interpreter's Dictionary of the Bible* have excellent comprehensive articles for the serious Bible student, though they may be more technical than many readers may desire. I have given a few interpretive and explanatory notes each day to help you understand the psalm in its historical and liturgical context.

One more prefatory note is needed. I have tried to be as inclusive as possible in my use of language. However, when referring to the speaker in each psalm, I have consistently used the masculine pronoun *he* for two reasons: one is the unfortunate fact that English lacks a gender-free, third-person singular personal pronoun; the other is that in ancient Israelite society out of which the psalms emerged, it is very unlikely that the author or speaker would have been female. To refer to the speaker as she, given the historical reality, would have struck an inauthentic and incongruous note. In other parts of the book that are not so historically time-bound, I have used both she and he when referring to a third party.

JUST AS MILLIONS OF FAITHFUL BELIEVERS through the centuries have found their prayer voice in the words of the psalms, so my hope is that in the course of this study, you will learn to sing the Lord's song in harmony with all those singers who have gone before us. In his book *Born after Midnight* A. W. Tozer states, "The world is big and tangled and dark, and we are never quite sure where true Christian[s] may be found. . . . The busy world may not even know [they] are there, except that they hear [them] singing." May these psalms become the songs that will sing in your heart through the brightest days and the darkest nights on your journey toward Mount Zion.

LARRY KALAJAINEN
Paris, France 1995

Week One

UP

Psalms of Praise and Presence

up *adv.* **1. a.** In or to a higher position. **8.** So as to advance, increase, or improve. **9.** With or to a greater intensity, pitch, or volume. **10.** Into a state of excitement or turbulence.

—**up** *adj.* **1.** Being above a former position or level; higher. **2.b.** Standing; erect. **c.** Facing upward. **3.** Raised; lifted. **4.** Moving or directed upward. **5.a.** Marked by increased excitement or agitation; aroused. **b.** *Informal.* Cheerful; optimistic; upbeat. **c.** *Slang.* Happily excited; euphoric. **6.** *Informal.* Taking place; going on.[3]

Now my head is lifted up above my enemies all around me.
—Psalm 27:6

UP IS WHERE ALL OF US LIKE TO BE. *Up* is normal and good. "I feel like a million bucks," or "I'm on top of the world" describe how we wish life were all the time. No one likes feeling down. We think that *up* is where life ought to be lived, so we spend a considerable amount of time, energy, and money keeping ourselves *up*.

Some of us have naturally buoyant personalities and our inherent optimism keeps us *up* most of the time. Others of us work harder at being *up*. When the blues strike or when unpleasant or painful situations confront us, we look around for diverting entertainment or activities that can cheer us up. A shop-till-you-drop expedition to the nearest mall; an evening watching mindless sitcoms on TV; a trip to the health club for a good workout; or, less beneficially, taking refuge in mind-altering drugs are a few ways we try to avoid being down and restore the feelings of being *up*.

Certainly many of life's experiences are *up* experiences. We all legitimately desire and need a sense of well-being. Yet to define normalcy exclusively in terms of being *up* is to embrace an illusion. Being *up* may be desirable, but it is not always possible. Life has other movements, other directions than *up*. Or, to shift the metaphor, life is not a unison melody consisting of a single line of notes in a major key. It is a rich polyphonic composition, full of variations and counterpoint in which the melody is interwoven with complex harmonies. The melody appears now in a bright allegro, now in a dark adagio, now in a sedate andante, and now in a galloping presto.

Nevertheless, *up* is where we want to be; the melody line is important, and it is our point of departure as well as our goal. The psalms in this section all have an *up* flavor about them. Praise or thanksgiving to God is a common element in them all, often the central element. Yet the praises sometimes strike us as being one-dimensional, naive, or even self-serving. We get the distinct impression that the singer in these songs may not have mastered the complexity of the composition yet.

We will discover that the full score demands that we learn different notes. Or, to return to our original metaphor, the journey from beginning to end is never in a straight line. We may begin at *up*, but the journey will involve abrupt descents, convoluted turnings, unmarked dead-ends, and boring pauses. When we eventually return to *up*, or when the melody reappears if you prefer, we will discover that though many of the landmarks look familiar, we are in a different place than where we started. It will be the journey itself, the movements and rhythms of the Spirit, that will reveal both the familiar and the new.

Preparation

Find a quiet place and a quiet time. Sit comfortably in whatever position will permit you to remain at rest and focused. With eyes closed, relax. Take five or six deep, slow breaths, silently breathing a prayer phrase such as *My God and my all.* Say, *My God* as you inhale. Hold that deep breath silently for a second or two, saying *and my all* as you exhale. Repeat this centering exercise until you feel any distractions you have brought with you ebbing away and a sense of inner quiet gaining strength. You may wish to extend this time by meditating on the following excerpt from the ancient Prayer of Manasseh, often called the *Kyrie Pantokrator*:

> *O Lord and Ruler of the hosts of heaven,*
>   *God of Abraham, Isaac, and Jacob,*
>   *and of all their righteous offspring:*
> *You made the heavens and the earth,*
>   *with all their vast array.*
> *All things quake with fear at your presence;*
>   *they tremble because of your power.*
> *But your merciful promise is beyond all measure;*
>   *it surpasses all that our minds can fathom.*
> *O Lord, you are full of compassion,*
>   *long-suffering, and abounding in mercy.*
>
> . . . .
>
>   *I will praise you without ceasing all the days of my life.*
> *For all the powers of heaven sing your praises,*
>   *and yours is the glory to ages of ages. Amen.*[4]

Scripture: Read Psalm 8.

The structure of this psalm is clear: verses 1-2 and 9 provide a frame for verses 3-8. The psalmist addresses the whole psalm to God. The framing statements at the beginning and at the end are exclamations of praise for God's majesty and sovereignty. The middle verses reveal that the praise springs from contemplation—not only of the wonders of God's creation—but more particularly, of the high status and godlike power of human beings as the pinnacles of that creative work.

Learning the Music

Most of us have had the experience of gazing at the stars on a clear night and feeling awed at the vast scale and apparent order of creation. Sometimes the wonders of creation have moved us to exclamations of praise. The psalmist begins with that upward look at the starry heavens but quickly draws our eyes back to earth. The starry heavens inspire the singer to find evidence of God's creative order and sovereign power closer at hand than the limitless reaches of space. It is human beings who inspire the psalmist to praise. Take a moment and think of a time when you have felt awe and wonder at God's creative work, particularly that work as revealed in humankind. You may wish to write about that moment and your feelings in the space below.

The psalmist sees evidence of God's majesty and greatness specifically in the fact that human beings have been given dominion over the works of God's hands. What do you think it means to have dominion? How have human beings—and you yourself—exercised this dominion? What is the difference, if any, between dominion and domination? Spend a few moments exploring these questions as they touch upon your own relationship, both to God and the creation.

Would a person with no financial means or a victim of discrimination be able to praise God as the psalmist does, contemplating the same reality? What does this suggest to you about the relationship between our circumstances and our ability and readiness to praise God? Is praise from the perspective of this psalm really praise of God, or is it self-praise?

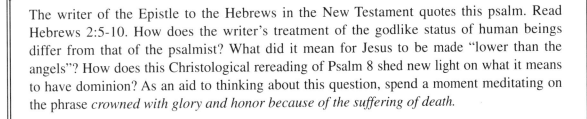

The writer of the Epistle to the Hebrews in the New Testament quotes this psalm. Read Hebrews 2:5-10. How does the writer's treatment of the godlike status of human beings differ from that of the psalmist? What did it mean for Jesus to be made "lower than the angels"? How does this Christological rereading of Psalm 8 shed new light on what it means to have dominion? As an aid to thinking about this question, spend a moment meditating on the phrase *crowned with glory and honor because of the suffering of death.*

With these new perspectives, pray the psalm aloud as a way of closing your quiet time today. How do your feelings about the psalm differ after this reflective study?

Singing the Song

Choose a current issue confronting our society, perhaps one that has perplexed you, that touches on the theme of human dominion. Try to discover ways in which your new understandings about what it means to exercise dominion can address that issue. Take some action that will give concreteness to those new understandings. It may take the form of a letter to your congressional representative or a change in your lifestyle or any number of things. But whatever you do concretely will enhance your praise of God.

Preparation

As you find your quiet place to spend these moments with God, try simply breathing the name of Jesus three or four times, taking deep breaths. This will help you put aside the distractions of the day. Then use this prayer of Lady Julian of Norwich to help you come to this time with a spirit that is centered and receptive to God's presence.

> *God, of your goodness give me yourself for you are sufficient for me. I cannot properly ask anything less, to be worthy of you. If I were to ask less, I should always be in want. In you alone do I have all.*[5]

Scripture: Read Psalm 18.

The title that appears above this psalm in most editions of the Bible indicates people's interpretation of the psalm at the time of its editing and inclusion in the psalter. The identical psalm, with minor variations, appears in 2 Samuel 22 as well. Whether the author of Samuel is quoting from Psalm 18 or vice versa is still a question of debate; whether or not David had any hand in its composition is unknown. What we do know is that the speaker in the psalm is a Davidic king rejoicing in his victory over his enemies in battle. The entire community used most, if not all, of the individual psalms in its various rituals and festivals.

Learning the Music

Verses 1-19 present a familiar scenario: A person whose life has just been threatened by death or disaster has been rescued. In his relief, he bursts forth into praise and thanksgiving to God, whom he perceives to be his rescuer. Vast relief expresses itself in exuberant and lyrical praise. Think about a time in your life when you too felt divinely rescued from danger or disaster. What were your sensations, your thoughts? To what or to whom did you attribute your rescue? How did you give expression to your feelings?

Verses 20-30 strike a different note. Here that first rush of vast relief and heartfelt thanksgiving to God, which follows on escape from disaster, gives way to a more self-aggrandizing appraisal of the situation. To what does the speaker in the psalm attribute his deliverance from disaster? In his view, why has God rescued him? When in your life have you translated a victory or a near-escape as a reward for your own moral goodness or superiority?

Verses 31-45 continue to emphasize the self-centered viewpoint of the speaker's relationship to God. The words *I*, *me*, or *my* occur more than twenty times in these verses. Observe some of the affirmations: "He trains my hands for war, . . . your help has made me great. . . . you made my assailants sink under me . . . . I beat them fine, like dust before the wind. . . . you made me head of the nations." If these and other statements in the text suggest that the speaker is confusing his own will and power with God's, what might these statements suggest about our tendency to do the same? When have you been able to convince yourself that what you wanted or your good fortune was also what God wanted? What might prevent such confusion?

The psalm ends with a ringing affirmation: "The Lord lives!" This phrase is less an assertion of God's existence than an affirmation of God's activity on behalf of the speaker. Not only has God delivered him from his enemies; God has caused him to be exalted over his enemies. What theology is implicit in this psalm? What can you affirm about the theology, and what about it makes you uneasy? If you can identify elements of triumphalism in your own life, reflect for some moments on what you might do to counteract it.

When you conclude your reflections, pray the psalm again. Let the affirmation "The Lord lives!" be one that you carry through the day in your consciousness, making you aware of how God is at work in your life and circumstances.

Singing the Song

As you watch the news, read the newspaper or news magazines, or listen to the speeches of political leaders or church leaders, listen for echoes of the theology expressed in this psalm. Where in your experience or in society do you encounter such a self-assured confidence that God is on our side because we're good people? Begin to think of ways in which you might encourage greater truth in dealing with issues where this sort of theology is present.

Day 3

Preparation

Take a few moments and recollect yourself, using the following prayer to remind yourself that wherever you are, and whatever you are doing, you are in God's presence:

> *Heavenly Father, in you we live and move and have our being: We humbly pray you so to guide and govern us by your Holy Spirit, that in all the cares and occupations of our life we may not forget you, but may remember that we are ever walking in your sight; through Jesus Christ our Lord. Amen.*[6]

Scripture: Read Psalm 26.

This psalm is a plea for vindication in the face of an unjust accusation. In verses 1-5, the psalmist pleads for God's vindication and asserts his innocence. Verses 6-7 describe a liturgical action: The washing of hands and the recitation of God's saving deeds dramatizes both the speaker's assertion of innocence and the righteousness of God. Verses 8-12 voice a plea for deliverance from harm resulting from the false accusation and an expression of confidence that the speaker's integrity provides a sure foundation for life.

Learning the Music

Think of a time when you were accused of doing or saying something, and you were innocent of the charge. How did you feel, and how did you respond?

Verses 4-5 sound a defensive note. The speaker not only asserts his innocence in the face of false accusation but emphasizes that he is a superior person, one who does not consort with those who are worthless and who are hypocrites. Why do you think we have a tendency to become defensive, adopting a posture of moral superiority when we are falsely accused? What in us makes us feel threatened by false accusations?

Dramatizing the plight of an accused innocent through liturgical acts and worship, the speaker recovers some equilibrium even though the issue is not resolved definitively. However at the close, the speaker can say, "My foot stands on level ground; in the great congregation I will bless the Lord." Try to think of the ways worship or prayer, particularly the recital of God's wondrous deeds in your past history (verse 7), have made a difference in your own feelings of outraged innocence. Where have you found the ability to regain your equilibrium? On what is such equilibrium based for the speaker in the psalm? for you?

Close your time of reflection by praying the psalm again. This time include a prayer for the ability to forgive those who have falsely accused you, especially if reconciliation has not yet occurred.

Singing the Song

Unfounded accusations against others are a common element in relationships, whether between individuals or groups of people. Such accusations are always damaging and sometimes deadly. Try to become aware of the number of times you yourself accuse others without full knowledge of the circumstances. Then begin noticing how many times newspaper or TV news accounts of strife between groups are based on accusations that each group hurls against the other. Consider whether the accusations are well-founded or sufficiently vague as to provoke reciprocal outrage or even violence.

Day 4

Preparation

From the Russian Orthodox tradition of spirituality comes a powerful tool for inner formation and centering known as the Jesus Prayer. It is a simple prayer designed to be repeated frequently until it becomes internalized to the point that, without conscious thought, one is praying without ceasing. Begin your time today by spending about three or four minutes quietly repeating this prayer: *Lord Jesus Christ, Son of God, have mercy on me.* You then may wish to pray the following prayer by John Wesley as your own for this day:

> *Thou art never weary, O Lord, of doing us good: Let us never be weary of doing thee service. But, as thou hast pleasure in the prosperity of thy servants, so let us take pleasure in the service of our Lord, and abound in thy work, and in thy love and praise evermore. O fill up all that is wanting, reform whatever is amiss, in us, perfect the thing that concerneth us. Let the witness of thy pardoning love ever abide in all our hearts.*[7]

Scripture: Read Psalm 52.

This psalm is classified as a lament, though it differs from most of the other laments in the psalter in that it does not begin with a plea for deliverance or a complaint that God is absent. Instead it launches immediately into a scathing attack on some person or party addressed sarcastically as "O mighty one." After cataloguing the enemy's sins (verses 1-4), the speaker in the psalm confidently predicts that God will bring about the utter downfall and ruin of this mighty one (verses 5-7). Then the speaker just as confidently proclaims his own well-being, a well-being derived from the fact that he, unlike his enemy, is righteous and trusts in God (verses 8-9). To us today, particularly Westerners, this assertion may seem arrogant or at least lacking in due regard for one's own moral failures or blameworthy motives. Yet people in the ancient Near East were not as introspective as people in modern Western culture. Behavior rather than motive revealed one's inner character; if one's behavior was correct, one was a person of integrity. Since one can measure and see behavior, it is not surprising that the speaker in the psalm could confidently assert his own integrity without hypocrisy.

Learning the Music

Obviously, something bad has happened to the speaker. He has been the victim of the intrigues of another person, the mighty one, whose sins are obvious and easily named. We do not know what damage the speaker has suffered; only that the tone of angry accusation is clear. The behavior that caused the harm apparently involves telling lies about the speaker.

All of us occasionally have been the victim of lies told about us. One of the results of being the victim of someone else's lie is that we feel powerless, and the powerlessness intensifies both the hurt and the anger we feel. Reflect on one such incident in your own experience. How does the angry accusation of the speaker and imputation of evil motives to the perceived betrayer strike you as being either similar or dissimilar to your own response? What sins did you lay at the other person's door? How did the act of accusing the other person and denouncing his or her behavior help you (or hinder you) in dealing with your feelings of powerlessness?

We often comfort ourselves in situations where we have felt betrayed by imagining retribution falling on our betrayer. The character Maude (played by Bea Arthur) on the old television show by the same name, used to say to her opponents, "God will get you for that." Does imagining God's justice falling on the other person offer us either a long-term balm for our hurt or a real expectation of redress? What does such a dire imprecation as "God will snatch and tear you from your tent; he will uproot you from the land of the living" do to the one who voices them? to the enemy against whom they are directed?

The speaker in the psalm describes himself as being like a green olive tree in the house of God. What feeling or self-understanding does such an image signify? Where does the speaker place his hope for a correct evaluation of his worth? Where do you place your hope when you are similarly accused?

What is the relationship between the angry denunciation of the other person's sins and the speaker's assertion of total trust in God? When have you tried to hold these two attitudes together in your own life? In what ways does this psalm offer you an adequate or inadequate model for resolving a conflict where you have been injured by lies?

Close your time in prayer today by being as honest as you can about your own feelings and behavior when you have felt betrayed by another person's untrue words. You may even want to pray this angry psalm as a way of honestly expressing those feelings to God. Then begin to let go of the anger against the other by praying for him or her.

Singing the Song

Think of a valued relationship in your life where lies have destroyed trust and inflicted pain. If you were the victim of the lie, begin to think of things you could do to break out of the pattern of angry denunciation and superficial confidence in your rightness. What concrete steps might you take to effect a reconciliation? This may demand a longer-term commitment than the time allotted for this day's exercise.

Preparation

Let this ancient prayer known as the *Phos hilaron* lead you into your worship today. It is a prayer for evening, but even if you are doing this exercise in the morning, you can join in the exuberance of its praises.

> *O gracious Light,*
> *pure brightness of the everliving Father in heaven,*
> *O Jesus Christ, holy and blessed!*
>
> *Now as we come to the setting of the sun,*
> *and our eyes behold the vesper light,*
> *we sing your praises, O God: Father, Son, and Holy Spirit.*
>
> *You are worthy at all times to be praised by happy voices,*
> *O Son of God, O Giver of life,*
> *and to be glorified through all the worlds.*[8]

Scripture: Read Psalm 92.

This is the only psalm in the entire psalter, whose title assigns it to a particular day. Its designation is A Song for the Sabbath Day. After an introduction in which the speaker affirms the appropriateness of giving thanks to God, the psalm naturally divides itself into three main segments. Verses 5-9 describe the fate of the wicked; verses 10-11 celebrate God's exaltation of the speaker over his enemies; and verses 12-15 affirm the prosperity of the righteous. Verse 4 may hold the key to the psalm's title. It specifically refers to "the works of your [God's] hands," that is, the creation. Since the Sabbath commemorates the completion of creation, the psalm celebrates that creative work.

Learning the Music

The psalmist sings, "It is good to give thanks to the Lord, . . . at the works of your hands I sing for joy." When was the last time you took time out (kept Sabbath) to contemplate God's works in creation and give praise? Reflect for a few moments on the relationship between the ability to praise God with joy and the deliberate taking of time away (Sabbath) from work and busy schedules for the contemplation of God's works. Focus particularly on your own

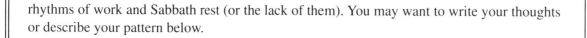

rhythms of work and Sabbath rest (or the lack of them). You may want to write your thoughts or describe your pattern below.

This contemplation of God's works, accompanied by praise, gives the psalmist a particular perspective on the fate of evildoers. On the one hand, the wicked sprout like grass, and all evildoers flourish. On the other hand, they are doomed to destruction forever. How do you evaluate the accuracy of this perspective? In what ways does it square with your own experience? A key to a deeper understanding of the psalmist's meaning may lay in his image of the wicked's sprouting like grass. What are some characteristics of sprouting grass?

The speaker concludes his evaluation of the fate of the wicked by saying, "For your enemies, O Lord, . . . shall perish." He then moves on to celebrate a personal deliverance that he attributes to God's favor and mercy: "My eyes have seen the downfall of my enemies." Is the speaker making a subtle, yet unmistakable, connection between *your* enemies, O Lord, and *my* enemies? What are the implications of this equation?

Think of a time when you have been under attack by enemies. How did you relate that situation to your relationship with God? If the speaker's (or your own) enemies had triumphed and the speaker (or you) had not been vindicated, how would this have affected your sense of God's justice or God's presence and care for you? What, if anything, does this psalm have to say about the tendency to attribute personal victories to God's intervention on our behalf, thus putting God squarely on our side?

The speaker contrasts the wicked who sprout and flourish like grass with the righteous who flourish like the palm tree and grow like a cedar in Lebanon. He interprets the fruitfulness (prosperity) of the righteous (among whom he obviously includes himself) as evidence of God's justice. How do you rate the accuracy of this comparison? Where in your own life or experience have you drawn similar conclusions?

This psalm has a rough honesty. Few of us could deny feeling that God was on our side when we have experienced a sense of triumphing over evildoers or enemies. Yet the facile equation of God's enemies with our enemies strikes us as self-serving, and the rather naive assumption that all the wicked are as transient as grass while all the righteous are as deeply rooted as trees doesn't really ring true. In fact, it often looks like the opposite is more accurate: The righteous get swept away in tides of violence while the wicked appear to prosper and flourish.

Yet the psalmist may know more than he (or we) thinks. In the last section of the psalm, the speaker says of the righteous, "They are planted in the house of the Lord; they flourish in the courts of our God." Spend a few moments reflecting on the relationship between the ultimate stability and prosperity of the righteous and the rootedness of the righteous in the community of faith. In other words, how do you relate faith and worship? How is your own life and your own ability to give thanks to God related to your rootedness (or lack of it) in a worshiping community?

Singing the Song

Begin to rethink the patterns of your own spiritual life. In particular, try to discover how much you base your spirituality on a naive belief that everyone should be up or happy. Try to identify superficial kinds of up experiences that you have come to depend on that may not stand up to the heat of the desert or the ferocity of the storms that have come, or will come, to you.

Spend some time reflecting on your relationship to a faith community. Are you a "Sunday-go-to-meetin'" type of person, for whom going to church is merely habitual? Are you a hit-or-miss worshiper, going to church when there's not something better or more interesting to do? Are you a church worker, always active and busy with church work but rarely taking time to reflect on the why of all that church busy-ness? Pray for discernment to understand and more fully participate in your faith community, understanding it to be the very source and wellspring of your ability to live on the up side of life. Give praise for the ultimate sovereignty of God, even when that sovereignty is not always apparent.

Group Session

The following suggestions are just that: suggestions. Do not feel constrained to follow all or any of them if another format or different discussion topics would be more useful for your group. Nor is the order of the suggestions for discussion particularly crucial; the numbers are merely for convenience of reference. Your group might spend the whole session on one of them or a shorter time on several of them.

Gathering

First and foremost, the Psalms are songs. They have served as one of the main wellsprings of the Christian musical tradition. Begin this first session by singing Psalm 8, the psalm with which this study began. The version found in *Hymns, Songs, and Spiritual Songs*, no. 162, sung to the tune Winchester Old is probably the most familiar. If you have a pianist, well and good; if not, anyone with a good sense of pitch and ability to carry a tune will be able to help the group sing this psalm.

Discussion

1. How did you respond to the thoughts about the *up* experiences of life? (If you need to refresh your memory, take a moment and scan the introduction to the first week's exercises again.) Did you agree or disagree with the writer's contention that most people think of up as normal, yet the up experience that is sought is often lacking in depth and complexity? You might want to share some personal stories to illustrate your response.

2. Which of the PREPARATION prayers were most meaningful to you personally?

3. What was the most important insight or new learning that you received from the daily exercises? Which psalm would you choose as your personal prayer? Why?

4. Which of the psalms from this past week did you find most personally challenging or difficult to comprehend? Which would you have difficulty praying as your own? Why?

5. Spend some time exploring the issue of honesty in prayer. How honest should we be in prayer? Are we willing to voice to God our ulterior motives, our self-centeredness, our vindictive attitudes toward enemies, or all the other human emotions we find in the psalms? Should we tell God we're angry at someone or that we hate someone or that we feel betrayed by someone? What does such honesty in prayer do to us personally and to our relationships with others?

Closing

Close by praying together Psalm 92, the psalm for the Sabbath.

DOWN

Psalms of Absence

‒‒‒‒‒‒‒‒‒‒‒‒‒‒‒‒‒‒‒‒

down *adv.* **1.a.** From a higher to a lower place or position. **b.** Toward, to, or on the ground, floor, or bottom. **7.a.** To or in a quiescent or subdued state. **b.** In or into an inactive or inoperative state. **8.** To or at a lower intensity. **9.** To or into a lower or inferior condition, as of subjection, defeat, or disgrace.

—**down** *adj.* **1.c.** Reduced; diminished. **2.** Afflicted; sick. **3.** Malfunctioning or not operating, especially temporarily. **4.** Low in spirits; depressed.

I am utterly bowed down and prostrate; all day long I go around mourning.
—Psalm 38:6

WITH AN ELOQUENT ECONOMY OF WORDS, the psalmist describes an experience common to us all. To be human is to know what it means to be utterly bowed down. The image the phrase *bowed down* conjures for us is of a peasant woman, bent over with the burden of a load of firewood on her back. She is flattened by the load.

For most people, this experience is episodic rather than continuous. Except for those suffering from persistent clinical depression, most of us experience times when we are *up* rather than *down*. We know that life has its highs as well as its lows. Yet the knowledge that life can be good and that happiness is possible is what makes the *down* times so painful. We know what we're missing.

Usually during those *down* times people feel not only emotionally flattened but spiritually flattened as well. God seems to be absent. The inner awareness or assurance of God's presence is gone. Our prayers become desperate cries for help or complaints that our lot is unfair. But even our prayers seem to stop at the ceiling over our heads. God does not appear to hear or even to care. Worse yet, we often stop praying altogether because we cannot bear to confront this seeming absence of God.

The psalms of lament strike a responsive chord in our experience. Some of the laments are deeply personal; others are more communal in nature. Some lament the absence of God in the life of the individual; others mourn God's absence from the life of the nation and society. All of them, however, deal honestly and poignantly with the human condition. Because of that honesty, they can offer us guidance when we are *down* and trying to find our way back up to the light.

Preparation

Take a few moments to quiet your mind and spirit. Sit comfortably in a quiet place where you will be free from external distractions. To lessen inner noise, use a prayer phrase such as *Jesus, Son of God, have mercy upon me*, or *O God, come to my assistance*, or *O Lord make haste to help me*, or another prayer of your own choosing. Repeat the phrase slowly, either aloud or in silence, for several minutes until you feel yourself becoming calm and centered. Then to help you prepare for the theme of this week's exercises, meditate for a few moments on the following prayer by Bishop Miles Coverdale:

> *O give us patience and steadfastness in adversity, strengthen our weakness, comfort us in trouble and distress, help us to fight; grant unto us that in true obedience and contentation of mind we may give over our own wills unto thee our Father in all things, according to the example of thy beloved Son; that in adversity we grudge not, but offer up ourselves unto thee without contradiction. . . . O give us a willing and cheerful mind, that we may gladly suffer and bear all things for thy sake.*[9]

Scripture: Read Psalm 6.

On the surface, Psalm 6 is a prayer for healing from a severe illness. However, throughout the history of prayer, persons have also viewed it as a prayer of penitence, interpreting the references to sickness as sickness of sin. The sick person begins by pleading with God not to punish him any longer (verses 1-3). He continues with a plea for healing based on the rationale that if death occurs, the speaker will be unable to praise God (verses 4-5). The speaker goes on to describe the sorrow and grief he experiences (verses 6-7). He concludes, abruptly shifting to a note of confidence that God has heard the speaker's prayer for healing which, when it occurs, will confound any enemies who would gloat over the speaker's downfall.

Linking God's wrath to sickness strikes many modern Christians as problematic, at least on an intellectual, theological level. At an emotional level, this link may still be common. There is no doubt that there is a link between sin and sickness. Yet most of us would feel uncomfortable about viewing all sickness in light of moral failure. The ancient Hebrews had no such hesitations, however. Confession of faith in the one God meant that all of life's experiences were related to that confession. So equating favorable circumstances with divine rewards for good behavior and sickness or trouble with divine punishment for bad behavior was easily accepted. Yet because this God served both individuals and the community that confessed faith in the one God, one could never rule out the possibility of a change in one's circumstances because of individual or community sin. One's circumstances could become the legitimate subject of prayer and even complaint.

One further important note for understanding is that while moderns tend to view sickness as an objective condition, curable or not by application of medical means, this psalm expresses the experience of being sick. Often modern medicine's concentration on treatment of strictly physical causes and procedures overlooks or suppresses the need for suffering to find words and be heard.

Learning the Music

How does the psalmist's assumption that his sickness is the result of God's wrath or discipline strike you personally? Reflect on a time when you have been seriously ill or deeply depressed. Were the feelings expressed in this psalm your feelings as well? Did you feel that you must have done something pretty bad to deserve what you were experiencing, or did you feel unfairly treated because you hadn't done anything bad enough to deserve what you were experiencing? How did that experience affect your feelings about God? about yourself? about your prayer life? Take a few moments and use the space below to reflect on your experience.

"My soul also is struck with terror, while you, O Lord—how long?" These words strike a poignant chord. One of the worst effects of being seriously ill is the fear that we have been forgotten or forsaken by God. In fact, any time of deep distress or trouble may trigger such feelings. Think of a time in your own life when you felt that God was absent. Consider times when the psalmist's plaintive question, "While you, O Lord—how long?" could have described your own feelings? Why do you think that God often seems absent in times of trouble? Why do you think God seemed absent to you?

Verses 6-7 graphically describe the depression that often accompanies serious illness or grief. Here the sufferer is observing his own suffering. What is there about serious illness or bereavement or depression that turns the focus onto oneself? What might this phenomenon say about the perceived absence of God?

The last few verses of this psalm suddenly introduce the presence of enemies. What connection do you make between personal suffering and enemies? What connection do you make between the sudden affirmation of confidence in the return of God's favor and this rebuking of enemies?

Close your time of reflection by praying the Lord's Prayer slowly, letting each petition have its due weight.

Singing the Song

Think of someone you know who is experiencing serious illness or bereavement. Find a way to let that person know that you are attentive to his or her need to be heard, to give voice to his or her experience. In other words, find a way to be available to this person, offering reassurance that God is present even in times of suffering and in those times when God seems absent.

Preparation

Meditate for several minutes on the following prayer. Let its petitions enter your inner being and become your own.

> *O God, make perfect my love toward Thee and to my Redeemer and Justifier; give me a true and unfeigned love to all virtue and godliness, and to all Thy chosen people wheresoever they be dispersed throughout all the world; increase in me strength and victory against all temptations and assaults of the flesh, the world, and the devil, that according to Thy promise I be never further proved or tempted than Thou wilt give me strength to overcome. Give me grace to keep a good conscience; give me a pure heart and mind, and renew a right spirit within me. Amen.*[10]

Scripture: Read Psalm 22.

Psalm 22 is the most important of eight psalms which are cited or alluded to in the stories of Jesus' passion in the Gospels. The opening words of this psalm are better known to Christian readers as Jesus' dying cry in Mark's Gospel as well as in Matthew's, which was based on Mark. Verse 18 of this psalm appears to have been transmuted by the author of Mark's Gospel into the story of the soldiers' gambling for Jesus' garment. Other details in the Gospel passion stories appear to be based on other Old Testament texts and psalms, particularly Psalms 31 and 69.

A modern reader, unfamiliar with the way ancient writers used the material of older sacred texts, might be troubled by the notion that the Gospel writers drew some details of the story of Jesus' passion from various Old Testament passages. This practice would not have bothered the first readers of the Gospels. Within Judaism persons often described and interpreted an event through a creative rereading and appropriation of older scriptures—particularly if the writer had not witnessed the event.

The narratives of Matthew, Mark, and Luke were constructed at least a generation after Jesus' crucifixion by persons who were not eyewitnesses. The preaching and storytelling of the first Christian communities gave ample testimony to the fact of Jesus' crucifixion, but the primary resources for understanding the meaning of that event were the Hebrew Scriptures. It was commonly understood, by both authors and readers, that citing a part of a text—such as Psalm 22:1—not only evoked the whole psalm in this case but the plight of the person in the psalm. In a very real sense, scripture helped create new scriptures. Much of the substance of the New Testament is the Old Testament reinterpreted and appropriated in light of the life, ministry, death, and resurrection of Jesus. At some point, you might read the passion narratives in the Gospels again after having read Psalms 22, 31, and 69 in order to develop a new appreciation for the way the writers employed this creative rereading and reinterpreting.

Learning the Music

In the first half of this psalm the speaker alternates between a consideration of his own predicament and a consideration of God's activity and relationship with both the speaker and his ancestors. The first section is a cry of despair and abandonment, "My God, my God, why have you forsaken me? . . . I cry by day, but you do not answer." As though shocked at the depth of his own despair, the speaker then argues that it is really not possible for God to abandon someone. He bases his argument on God's past faithfulness: "Yet you are holy. . . . In you our ancestors trusted, and you delivered them." If you can find an echo in your own experience of this rebounding between the feelings of abandonment and belief in God's faithfulness, reflect for a few moments on that vacillation between despair and confidence, outrage and trust. What causes such extreme swings in our feelings?

"But I am a worm, and not human; scorned by others" describes an emotional state that we moderns might call low self-esteem. Such feelings of negative self-worth are common in the midst of a severe trial or tragedy. Think of a time when you or someone close to you have had such feelings. What may have caused them? How did you or the other person deal with them? Reflect on the relationship between feelings of worthlessness and feelings that God is absent. In what ways are the two connected?

How does the speaker's description of his plight in verses 14-18 connect with your own experiences of desolation? When have you had similar feelings of depression and paranoia? How did you feel about God at that time? What was the connection, as you understand it, between your emotional state and your sense of God's presence or absence?

From verse 19 on, the mood of the psalm changes from one of vacillation between abandonment and remembrance to one of a determined plea for God's help and the actual praise of God's glory, sovereignty, and faithfulness. The speaker appears to have reached a decision to trust God even in the midst of depression and despair. He vows to offer formal thanksgiving when God delivers him from his predicament. The speaker gives no single reason for the decision to trust and praise. However, the earlier vacillation hints at what may have produced this shift. At certain moments, the speaker remembered God's past faithfulness: "In you our ancestors trusted . . . and you delivered them. . . . It was you who took me from the womb; you kept me safe on my mother's breast." How do remembrance and recital relate to the ability to transcend one's own despair, moving to trust in God? For the speaker, this recital takes place in the midst of the congregation, in the presence of brothers and sisters. What does this suggest to you about the importance of a caring faith community in rising out of depression to hope? When has such an experience of community been important to you?

To close your time of meditation, spend a few moments remembering. Remember your experiences of God's presence and God's faithfulness, of persons and events that you recognized as an answer to your prayers. Allow those remembrances to begin shaping your present circumstances, even those that are difficult or dark.

Singing the Song

Begin looking around you, especially in your circle of family or friends, and take notice of anyone in that circle who appears to be going through deep depression or despair, someone who may feel abandoned. Try to discover ways in which you may be the agent of remembrance and therefore of hope, not in a preachy manner from a position of superior faith but in an incarnational way, where you become the caring faith community for the other person.

Day 8

Preparation

Many Christians have found it helpful to prepare themselves mentally and spiritually for prayer by simply sitting in silence and gazing at a lighted candle, a cross or crucifix, or a painted icon. Focus on the object for several minutes without actively thinking about it; simply let its significance as a symbol seep into your awareness as you gaze at it steadily. This concentrated gaze without active thought is a way to lessen the outward distractions of noises in the house or in the street as well as inner distractions such as thoughts of one's daily schedule or family problems. We gain an inner sense of stillness that is necessary to hear the still small voice of God. You may want to try this method of centering to prepare for your time of meditation and prayer today. You also may want to spend some moments meditating on this prayer for healing, particularly if you are experiencing a time of sickness or pain; or you may simply want to have it as a resource for some future time of need.

> *Lord Jesus Christ, by your patience in suffering you hallowed earthly pain and gave us the example of obedience to your Father's will: Be near me in my time of weakness and pain; sustain me by your grace, that my strength and courage may not fail; heal me according to your will; and help me always to believe that what happens to me here is of little account if you hold me in eternal life, my Lord and my God. Amen.*[11]

Scripture: Read Psalm 88.

This psalm is, perhaps, the saddest in the whole psalter. It is a personal lament, unrelieved by the shift from complaint to hope found in most of the other laments in the psalter. In fact, verse 2 voices the only petition. The rest of the psalm is a catalogue of troubles, centered on the nearness and finality of death. The speaker says that he has been wretched and close to death from his youth. We do not know whether the speaker's affliction is a lifelong disease or physical disability, or simply the black hole of depression.

In earlier Judaism, death was conceived primarily in negative terms: there was no concrete image of an afterlife, only an image of the absence of life. The grave, Sheol, the Pit, Abaddon are all synonyms for the location of the dead, who exist—if it can be called existence—only as shades, not really possessing life but merely the faded echo of life. The implied answer to all the rhetorical questions in verses 10-12 is no. No, the dead do not praise God. No, God does not work saving acts on behalf of the dead. No, God's steadfast love is not proclaimed in the grave. No, God does not even remember the dead.

If it does nothing else, this psalm reminds us that parts of the Bible are pre-Christian though other passages from the Hebrew Scriptures offer a different perspective. (See Job

19:25-26 or Ps. 49:13-15.) In this psalm we do not find Paul's confidence that in our death we participate in, and are transformed by, the death and resurrection of Jesus. Not here, Paul's bold statement that "if the earthly tent we live in is destroyed, we have a building from God, not made with hands, eternal in the heavens" (2 Cor. 5:1-2). Nor do we find the notion asserted by the author of First Peter that Jesus "was put to death in the flesh, but made alive in the spirit, in which also he went and made a proclamation to the spirits in prison [that is, the dead] (1 Pet. 3:18-19). What we do have is a pathetically accurate description of hopelessness and anguish of spirit, a state to which most human beings succumb at some point, even if temporarily.

Learning the Music

Have you ever experienced the unrelenting hopelessness expressed in this psalm? (If you cannot personally identify with the feelings expressed, perhaps you can think of a close friend or a family member who has gone through such an experience.) Did your (or your friend's) hopelessness have a tangible cause? Was it related to identifiable circumstances such as bereavement or physical illness; or did it appear to have deeper emotional, spiritual, or psychological roots? What were your feelings (or your friend's, if you were made aware of them) about God during this time of deep anguish of soul? Why does such deep depression make us feel as though God has forgotten us or put us in the depths of the Pit? What might this tell us about our images of God?

The speaker obviously subscribes to the theology, common in earlier Hebrew thought, that God is punishing him for some sin, though he never names the sin. "You have put me in the depths of the Pit. . . . Your wrath lies heavy upon me" (verses 6-7). This implicit theology of misfortune or sickness as God's punishment for evil is not uncommon today, even in a Christian context. You may remember having had similar notions at some point yourself. What is the continuing appeal of a theology of direct divine retribution? What does this theological understanding say about us? about God? What effect does such a theology, whether implicit or explicit, have upon our relationship with God? with other people? with ourselves?

In the closing statement, the speaker says, "You have caused friend and neighbor to shun me; my companions are in darkness." The disruption of social relationships is often one of the results of personal tragedy, anguish, or depression. Why do personal troubles often seem to cut us off from the very persons who could help us? Reflect on a time when you felt cut off from friends and neighbors, or even your own family. Who was responsible for the alienation? What connection do you see, if any, between the alienation we feel from other people and the alienation we feel from God? Conversely, what connection do you see between the care we receive from others and our feelings that God cares for us?

Despite his being mired in hopeless despair, the speaker is able to address his complaint to God. Prayer is the medium the speaker uses to voice this lament. What does this suggest to you about the uses of prayer? What value might brutal honesty have in prayer? Would you dare to confess such hopelessness to God?

If you are currently going through a depressing or deeply distressing time, you may want to use this psalm to give voice to your own feelings, letting God know and letting yourself know, just how bad you feel. Or you may think of a friend or family member whose plight this psalm describes, and you may want to use this psalm as a way of empathizing with his or her experience. But don't allow this psalm to be your whole prayer. Instead, close your time by meditating for a few moments on what we, as followers of Christ, know about God's care for us. You may want to read Matthew 6:25-33 or 1 Corinthians 15:12-28 as a way of moving beyond the experience of bleak despair.

Singing the Song

If you know someone who is experiencing feelings similar to those of the speaker in the psalm, begin to think and pray about ways you could be an agent of hope. Try to imagine some concrete ways you could demonstrate that God is not absent but present and actively at work. In other words, what kind of caring could you render that would help the other person begin to sense God's caring?

Day 9

Preparation

Again begin your time by gazing at an icon or lighted candle or some other object that may symbolize God's presence. If you are not used to this technique for entering into inner quietness or stillness, it may take some time to feel comfortable with it. After some moments, meditate on this prayer by François Fénelon as a way of preparing to read another passion psalm:

Lord, I know not what I ought to ask of you; you alone know what I need; you love me better than I know how to love myself. O Father! give to your child that which I know not how to ask. I dare not ask either for crosses or consolations: I simply present myself before you, I open my heart to you. Behold my needs which I know not myself; see and do according to your tender mercy. Smite, or heal; depress me or raise me up: I adore all your purposes without knowing them; I am silent; I offer myself in sacrifice: I yield myself to you; I would have no other desire than to accomplish your will. Pray yourself in me. Amen.[12]

Scripture: Read Psalm 69.

This psalm is also a lament, cast in the form of a prayer for deliverance from powerful enemies. As in most of the psalms, there is no clear indication of the historical identity of the speaker. It may be a king, since the traditional ascription is "Of David." Some scholars have suggested that Jeremiah fits the speaker's profile, and it is likely that the psalm originated in or around the time of Jeremiah's ministry. However, discovering the identity of the speaker is not an important issue.

The psalm evokes the universal human experience of being victimized by false accusations and the manipulations of one's enemies. Verses 1-29 constitute the lament proper. Here the speaker intersperses pleas for God's help with descriptions of the enemies' evil deeds against the speaker. At one point, the speaker breaks into an angry prayer asking God to curse and destroy his enemies. At verse 30 the psalm decisively shifts from lament to praise. Here the speaker strongly reaffirms his belief that God is the source, not only of his own salvation but the salvation of God's people as well.

The early Christians reread this psalm, like Psalm 22, in light of their experience of Jesus' death and resurrection. (You may want to review the comments about Psalm 22 in the exercise for Day 7.) They did not believe that the psalmist had predicted Jesus' passion; rather the psalm gave a language, a voice, and a perspective to those struggling to understand the events of Jesus' passion in hindsight. It served as one of their interpretive keys. The writers of the New Testament refer to this psalm seventeen times. For example, all the Gospel writers cite verse 21 in their accounts of Jesus' crucifixion, and John's Gospel quotes verse 9 as an interpretive aid in the story of Jesus driving the moneychangers out of the Temple. Though the imprecations upon the enemies hardly fit our picture of Jesus, the writer of Acts did see verse 25 as an apt caption to describe the fate of Judas Iscariot (Acts 1:20).

Learning the Music

The opening verses of this psalm have a surprisingly contemporary ring to them, "Save me, O God, for the waters have come up to my neck." Think of the expression we often use when we are frustrated, hurt, and angered to the limit of our endurance: "I've had it up to here!" (usually accompanied by a motion indicating our chin or neck or eyebrows). A key to the feelings of angry frustration that emerge is the speaker's assertion (verse 4) that he is hated without cause. Why can we bear up under many difficulties without becoming angry if we perceive those difficulties as impersonal or not maliciously caused (such as a diagnosis of a serious health problem or an accident), but when we suspect we are being treated shabbily, we become frustrated and angry at once?

Many of us have complained to others or to God about our unfair treatment. However, the speaker adds a note of honest self-appraisal to his complaint, "O God, you know my folly; the wrongs I have done are not hidden from you." Reflect for a few moments on your own patterns of anger and frustration when things are not going well. Is your own style of lament self-justifying or confessional? What difference does it make?

The speaker begins telling God that he is suffering the insults of his enemies because of his faithfulness and devotion to God, evidenced by his piety in fasting. It is almost as though he is blaming God for his enemies' actions. What comfort does it give us when we suffer, to feel that we are martyrs to truth or goodness, suffering innocently at the hands of the wicked? Is such a sentiment honest, or is it an expression of self-pity? Whose will is really

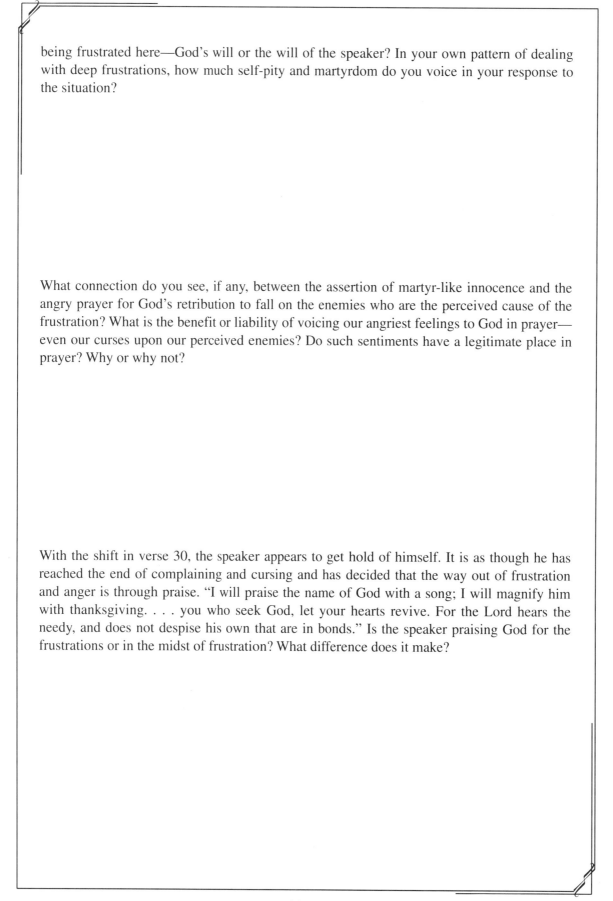

being frustrated here—God's will or the will of the speaker? In your own pattern of dealing with deep frustrations, how much self-pity and martyrdom do you voice in your response to the situation?

What connection do you see, if any, between the assertion of martyr-like innocence and the angry prayer for God's retribution to fall on the enemies who are the perceived cause of the frustration? What is the benefit or liability of voicing our angriest feelings to God in prayer— even our curses upon our perceived enemies? Do such sentiments have a legitimate place in prayer? Why or why not?

With the shift in verse 30, the speaker appears to get hold of himself. It is as though he has reached the end of complaining and cursing and has decided that the way out of frustration and anger is through praise. "I will praise the name of God with a song; I will magnify him with thanksgiving. . . . you who seek God, let your hearts revive. For the Lord hears the needy, and does not despise his own that are in bonds." Is the speaker praising God for the frustrations or in the midst of frustration? What difference does it make?

What relationship do you see between frustration and anger on the one hand and praise of God on the other? In what ways might the angry prayer of cursing and complaint have enabled the speaker's shift to praise? In other words, is it possible to praise God as a way out of our frustration and anger if we are not totally honest with God about that anger?

Close your time today by praying for your worst enemy. Begin by letting God know all the anger, hurt, and frustration you feel as a result of the wrong you perceive has been done to you. Be honest in your own self-appraisal. Then begin to praise God, even if you don't feel like praising. You may even want to sing a favorite hymn of praise.

Singing the Song

As you relate to colleagues, classmates, your children, parents, or spouse, try to keep track of how many times you place them in the position of enemies who cause your frustration. Also note how frequently you hear those around you naming others as their enemies. Try to imagine how you could become the means through which they could make the shift from frustrated anger to praise.

Day 10

Preparation

Spend a few moments withdrawing from the distractions of your day. Use either a prayer phrase such as the Jesus Prayer or a favorite scripture sentence, or again use an icon or other object to draw your focus inward. Then pray this prayer:

> *O God, your never-failing providence sets in order all things both in heaven and earth: Put away from us, we entreat you, all hurtful things, and give us those things which are profitable for us; through Jesus Christ our Lord, who lives and reigns with you and the Holy Spirit, one God, for ever and ever. Amen.*[13]

Scripture: Read Psalm 102.

The psalm's title is "A prayer of one afflicted [Heb. *'ani*], when faint and pleading before the Lord." We may translate *'ani* as "the afflicted or weak," a common designation of one half of a pair of opposites often found in the scriptures. The other half is "the strong or the mighty." One who is afflicted or weak has no one to depend upon for help but God. The strong or the mighty depend upon no one but themselves, and they are the oppressors of the weak. In this psalm, the speaker identifies with the weak. The speaker emphasizes both his mortality and utter helplessness on the one hand and the eternity and sovereign power of God on the other. The movement between these two realities provides the psalm's structure.

Learning the Music

In verses 3-11, the speaker uses a variety of similes to describe his plight: like smoke, like a furnace, like grass, like an owl of the wilderness, like a lonely bird, eat ashes like bread, like an evening shadow. Take a few moments and explore each of these images. What feeling is the speaker describing in each? What single word would you choose to describe the emotional state imaged by all these similes taken together? Which of the images speak most powerfully to you or resonate with similar feelings or circumstances of life that you have experienced? Or, to put it another way, what time or experience in your own life corresponds most closely to the experience described by the speaker?

When we are young, we feel immortal; when we reach middle age, we become more keenly aware of our mortality. The speaker has reached middle age. In his evocative description, "My days are like an evening shadow," and in his plaintive petition in verse 24, "O my God, do not take me away at the mid-point of my life," we see a stark portrait of a person confronting the inevitability, and perhaps, even the imminence of life's end. It appears that some crisis, a sudden illness or reversal or bereavement, has precipitated the speaker's contemplation of human mortality. Why do you think that crises, particularly those that come upon us in midlife, cause us to reflect on life's end? Why should this knowledge come to us as a shock rather than as a natural awareness within us at all times?

In ancient times, monarchs who were celebrating triumphs and conquests sometimes instructed slaves to whisper in their ear at the height of the celebrations, "Remember, that you too are mortal and shall one day be dust." Reflect on your own awakening to your mortality, if you have had such an awakening. What precipitated it? How did you react? How did it change your manner of life or thought?

"But you, O Lord, are enthroned forever. . . . Let this be recorded for a generation to come, so that a people yet unborn may praise the Lord. . . . They [the heavens and the earth] will perish, but you endure." For the speaker, the answer to his deep depression brought on by the contemplation of his own mortality is the eternal sovereignty of God. This eternity is not a static state of being, however. The eternal God is eternally active: hearing the groans of the prisoners, setting free those doomed to die. The speaker turns his thoughts away from his own frailty to a contemplation of God's eternal, saving faithfulness and finds peace. What clue do these verses offer for dealing with your own experiences of depression or fears of mortality? How would it make a difference in your own life to focus on God's eternity and saving faithfulness rather than on your own problems or fears of mortality?

Close your time today by praying through the psalm again, identifying with the speaker as much as you can—through the movement from despair or depression to calmness of spirit in view of God's eternity and faithfulness.

Singing the Song

As you watch television, read the newspapers or magazines, or observe the actions of people around you, try to find evidence of anxiety in the face of mortality. Where do you see the fear of death manifested in daily life, both in your own and in others' lives? Then begin to think about how you could become a reminder of God's eternal faithfulness so that those close to you, who appear to be living in the shadow of death, might see the possibilities for their own peace.

Group Session

Gathering

This past week's psalms have been singularly depressing in tone. Sickness, personal crises, fears of mortality, attacks by enemies—real or imagined: All are common human experiences, and all have been given voice in prayer. Yet somewhat surprisingly, few of these "down" psalms have found their way into the hymnody of the church. One might think that people do not want to sing about depression or tragedy or loss, yet a brief glance at the world of popular music demolishes that notion. One only has to think of the vast number of popular, country-western, or rock songs that speak of heartbreak, the pain of unrequited love, or even death. Yet relatively few hymns deal with these unpleasant realities of life.

A quick search through the hymnals of the Church of England, the Presbyterian Church in the United States, or The United Methodist Church turned up a setting of only one of the psalms for this week, Psalm 22 (*Hymns, Psalms, and Spiritual Songs*, 168). If you have access to it, you may want to sing it. Many hymnals carry Martin Luther's setting of Psalm 130, "Out of the Depths I Cry to You." It also gives voice to the experience of life at the bottom.

Discussion

1. Did you find that the psalms for this week spoke to your life experience, or did you feel that they were stylized exaggerations?

2. Which of the psalms spoke most eloquently to your own down experiences? Why? With which did you have the most difficulty identifying?

3. Do you find it easy or difficult to give voice in prayer to your deepest sorrows or most depressing experiences? How have your own down times found expression in your prayers up to this point? How have this week's exercises either reinforced or changed your own patterns of relating to God?

4. In reflecting on your own experiences of God's absence, do you have a tendency to withdraw from contact with other people at such times, or do you seek out other people? What connection, if any, do you see between the presence of other people and the presence of God during the down times of life?

5. Why do fewer hymns express the painful or depressing experiences of life rather than faith, confidence, or praise? Does this fact suggest a possible reason why many people prefer popular music to hymns? If so, what does this say about our notions of spirituality?

Closing

To close the group session, spend a few moments in silence reflecting again on the second movement in Psalm 102, the psalm for Day 10. Direct your thoughts and your spirit to the eternity and faithfulness of God. Then pray the whole psalm together aloud.

Week Three

THROUGH

Psalms of Struggle and Growth

through *prep.* **1.** In one side and out the opposite or another side of. **2.** Among or between; in the midst of. **4.b.** Into and out of the handling, care, processing, modification, or consideration of. **6.** From the beginning to the end of. **7.** At or to the end of; done or finished with, especially successfully.

—through *adv.* **1.** From one end or side to another or an opposite end or side. **2.** From beginning to end; completely. **3.** Throughout the whole extent or thickness; thoroughly. **4.** Over the total distance; all the way. **5.** To a conclusion or an accomplishment.

—through *adj.* **2.b.** Continuing on a highway without exiting.

idiom. **through and through. 1.** In every part; throughout. **2.** In every aspect.

> When through the deep waters I call thee to go,
> the rivers of woe shall not thee overflow;
> For I will be with thee, thy troubles to bless,
> and sanctify to thee thy deepest distress.
> —*The United Methodist Hymnal,* no. 529

"SHE'S REALLY BEEN THROUGH IT, lately. I don't know how she stands it."
"He's been through hell and back these past few weeks."
"Some things you can't escape; you just have to go through them."
We commonly use all of these expressions to talk about our own or others' difficult passages. Once the immediate shock of the plunge from the heights to the depths passes, we discover ourselves in new territory. We're not *up*; we're still *down*. But *down* is not a static state of being. *Down* has movement; we are going *through* something—grieving, depression,

illness, anxiety, dysfunctional relationships, traumas—the list could go on and on, just as the trouble we're experiencing appears to go on and on.

That going on and on is a part of the spiritual journey that all of us face sooner or later. Yet this sustained passage through whatever it is that has precipitated our plunge from *up* to *down* is not a passive, detached, and smooth ride. The road is rocky here; the bumps are frequent and jarring. Pain is often a constant companion, whether it be physical, emotional, or spiritual pain or a combination of all three. There are dead ends, wrong turnings, and much retracing of our steps until we find the right path. But the path always leads *through*, not around or over.

THIS SPIRITUAL MAP REFERENCE called *through* is a place of conversion. Conversion is the transformation of our wills so that they are in harmony with God's will. Conversion is not a once-in-a-lifetime experience. If it were, then theoretically as soon as we were converted, we would have no more problems. From that point on, life would be smooth sailing. But because there are depths of our being of which we are never fully aware at any one point in our lives and because spiritual maturity is not an instant attainment but a lifelong process, conversion will always be necessary. As new facets of my own deep-rooted self-will and resistance to God are brought to light in the painful passages of life, they will need to be converted. Conversion is always accompanied by repentance. Repentance simply means that we recognize that we've taken a wrong turn, we've wandered down a cul-de-sac, we've fallen into a deep hole, and we need to turn around and retrace our steps to the true path.

The difficulty is that repentance and conversion are not easy or necessarily pleasant. The process is often costly and painful. Facing up to our shortcomings, our inadequacies, our failures, and our sins is costly. It hurts to acknowledge the reality of who we are. Yet without a willingness to pay the price or bear the hurt, there is no growth, no moving on to spiritual maturity. In the spiritual life, as in athletics, the slogan "no pain, no gain" is accurate, if not desirable.

THE PSALMS IN THIS SECTION ARE PSALMS that may provide some models for us when we are *down* and going *through* our times of struggle and growth. All of them are cries for help. What makes them different from the psalms in last week's exercises is that they do not simply express the experience of plunging down into depression, illness, bereavement, or betrayal. They show evidence of struggle to find meaning, to find a way forward in the midst of the depression or pain. They reflect an honesty about self and sin and a fervent desire to recover the assurance of God's presence. That struggle, that quest, is so intense at times that it takes on the character of combat with God. As Jacques Ellul says in his book *Prayer and Modern Man*, "Prayer is this demand that God not keep silence. . . . Whoever wrestles with God in prayer puts his [or her] whole life at stake. Otherwise it would not be a *genuine* combat, or indeed it would not be a combat *with God*."

The very notion of prayer as struggle presumes that God is going *through* our struggles with us. Struggles, growing pains, conversions are always more bearable when we know we're not alone. So persevere. Go *through*. The end of the journey is not yet.

Preparation

Many people find that music prepares them inwardly for prayer. For some, the hymns of Christian worship play an important role in their spirituality. Others who have not had exposure to the church's hymnody may be moved spiritually by other kinds of music— perhaps a symphony recording or the songs of a particular singer. You may wish to come to your prayer time today accompanied by music. Sing or hum a favorite hymn, or listen to a recording that makes you feel contemplative or drawn toward God. Then use the following prayer of Susanna Wesley, the devout mother of John and Charles Wesley, founders of the movement known as Methodism:

> *You, O Lord, have called us to watch and pray. Therefore, whatever may be the sin against which we pray, make us careful to watch against it, and so have reason to expect that our prayers will be answered. In order to perform this duty aright, grant us grace to preserve a sober, equal temper, and sincerity to pray for your assistance. Amen.* [14]

Scripture: Read Psalm 55.

Some scholars see evidence that there are parts of two psalms joined together here, with parts of the psalm speaking of general moral disintegration and the wicked who are enemies of the righteous, while other parts lament the wounds caused by one particular enemy who was formerly a close friend. But while the psalm may be a composite, there is no clear division between the two emphases. Often a personal betrayal or slight provokes a larger, gloomy meditation on the declining moral condition in general. It is a short step from *my* enemy to *the* enemies.

Learning the Music

The psalm opens with a plea that God pay attention to the speaker's plight and do something about it. Such a plea is a common form of address to God. Undoubtedly you've heard someone address God in a similar fashion; perhaps you have done it yourself. Why in times of trouble, do we often feel that God is not paying attention to us and needs such a reminder?

Examine such a time in your own life when you felt that God wasn't paying attention to you. Why did you feel that way?

The speaker, in the midst of deep feelings of anguish and fear, longs for wings like a dove in order to fly away and be at rest. When have you felt so overburdened by your troubles that you would have given anything to escape from them? Why do we wish to be disengaged from life when life becomes difficult? What is the nature of the troubles that are likely to make us feel this way?

In verse 12, after decrying the moral wickedness within the city, a sudden shift reveals the true nature of the speaker's anguish. An intimate friend has betrayed him: "My companion laid hands on a friend and violated a covenant with me with speech smoother than butter but with a heart set on war; with words that were softer than oil, but in fact were drawn swords." What connection do you see, if any, between a deep, personal hurt and the perception that the whole world is going to the dogs? Reflect on a time when you have known such a painful betrayal by someone close to you: a friend, a family member, a colleague. How did that experience affect, not only your feelings about your friend, but your view of life and the moral state of the world in general?

In verses 16-23, the speaker oscillates between affirmations of trust in God and angry, vengeful denunciations of the familiar enemy: "But I call upon God, and the Lord will save me. . . . God . . . will hear, and humble them. . . . Cast your burden on the Lord, and [the Lord] will sustain you. . . . But you, O God, will cast them down into the lowest pit. . . . But I will trust in you." When have you experienced such vacillations between outraged hurt, vengeful anger, and the belief that God will help you? Why do the hurts suffered at the hands of intimate enemies wound us so much more deeply than the hurts suffered at the hands of strangers? Why can we often forgive and forget injuries inflicted by strangers, but those inflicted by the betrayal of a friend or loved one we cannot, or will not, let go? Why do we expect that God will take our part?

Close your time by spending some moments quietly repeating these lines from the psalm: "Cast your burden on the Lord and [the Lord] will sustain you." After meditating on that line for some time, bring the hurt that you have suffered from an intimate enemy into God's presence and let God begin to take that burden from your shoulders. If you can, at this stage, begin to pray for the strength to let go of the hurt and forgive the one who inflicted it.

Singing the Song

As you go out to face your day or prepare to face the next day after sleeping, begin to think of ways in which you might initiate a process of reconciliation with someone who has wounded you deeply. Remember that reconciliation does not mean pretending that no injury ever occurred. Both parties must acknowledge the wrong and explore its full significance before effecting reconciliation. Do not leap into a reconciliation attempt without thinking the situation through carefully, but begin to formulate a course of action. The important thing is to take the initiative.

Day 12

Preparation

Again you may wish to use a hymn or other music to prepare yourself for your time of prayer and meditation on the psalms. You also may wish to use the following prayer, noting particularly the petition for God's help in passing through things temporal:

O God, the protector of all who trust in you, without whom nothing is strong, nothing is holy: Increase and multiply upon us your mercy; that, with you as our ruler and guide, we may so pass through things temporal, that we lose not the things eternal; through Jesus Christ our Lord, who lives and reigns with you and the Holy Spirit, one God, for ever and ever. Amen.[15]

Scripture: Read Psalm 137.

This lament, unlike many others in the Psalms, refers to a specific and recognizable historical event: the conquest and destruction of Jerusalem by King Nebuchadnezzar of Babylon and his Edomite allies in 587 B.C. The speakers are the exiles who have been deported from Judea and who now sit along the banks of the Tigris and Euphrates, longing for their homeland. The psalm naturally divides itself into three sections. In the first section (verses 1-3), the exiles give voice to their grief as they remember Zion (that is, Jerusalem). In the second, they pledge their undying faithfulness to the memory of their homeland, even to the point of calling down a curse upon themselves if they forget who they are and what Jerusalem means to them. The third section opens with a plea that God will remember the day of Jerusalem's fall and wreak a terrible vengeance on those who destroyed it.

Learning the Music

All of us, when we are in the down times of life, can remember when life was better. We can remember how happy we were, and our memories serve to reinforce how miserable we are now. Can you identify your Zion or Jerusalem? What is the remembered standard by which you measure your present happiness or unhappiness? Where are the symbolic rivers of Babylon for you? What experience or circumstances represents exile, loss, and painful memories of a happier time?

If you have ever felt what the exiles felt ("How could we sing the Lord's song in a foreign land?"), describe that feeling and try to identify what made you feel so hopeless or alone. Why is it hard to sing the Lord's song in a foreign land? (Think of the term *foreign land* as a metaphor for any experience in which we feel driven out or exiled from our normal happiness or feeling of being at home.) What connection do you see between the ability to sing the Lord's song and the sense of being alienated or downcast?

Why, when we are experiencing alienation or the feeling of being lost, do we often feel the need to pledge ourselves to faithfulness to some remembered golden time or place of the past? The intensity of this feeling expressed by the speakers in the psalm is seen in the fact that they call down a curse on themselves if they should get comfortable in Babylon and forget Jerusalem. What do they fear? Where can you identify this need to pledge yourself to remember something that is past? What effects of such a pledge can you identify in your life?

When the memory of the lost homeland is at its most intense, the need for vengeance against those who caused the exiles' loss asserts itself: "Remember, O Lord, against the Edomites the day of Jerusalem's fall." What connection, if any, do you see between hanging on to the past and hanging on to resentments and hatreds? It is all too easy to identify this syndrome of remembrance of wrongs and perpetuation of hatred and violence when it pertains to nations or peoples. It is not as easy to see it in ourselves at the personal level. Spend a few moments examining your resentments and hatreds. To which remembrances are they connected? What fears may be hidden within the resentment and hatred? Confessing fear and resentment becomes a step in healing.

Close your time today by remembering. But instead of remembering what was but is no more and the wrongs done to you that contributed to that loss, remember God's faithfulness to you in the past. Remember the good that God brought through other people during past times of difficulty or alienation. Remember that, for Israel, even in Babylon, God's steadfast love was at work. Remember that God's steadfast love is at work in your Babylon as well. As you remember that covenant faithfulness, which is never confined to Jerusalem but is present even in Babylon, give thanks to God and pray for the Babylonians and Edomites in your life.

Singing the Song

As you read your newspaper and watch the news on television, try to identify where in the world around you this syndrome of remembrance and vengeance is being acted out. Then look closer to home. Where in your community (city, neighborhood, church) do you see this pattern? Begin to identify ways in which you can help transform memories of past wrongs to memories of God's faithfulness in the midst of wrong.

Day 13

Preparation

Again make use of a prayer phrase such as *Jesus, Light of the World, illumine me* or *Jesus, Bread of Life, feed me*. Repeat the first part as you breathe in and the last part as you breathe out. Do this for several minutes until you feel the sense of inner quiet begin to replace inner noise. To prepare yourself for today's theme, you might want to meditate for a few moments on this prayer by Mechtild of Magdeburg who was struggling to be faithful while feeling spiritually empty and devoid of God's presence:

> *Lord, since thou hast taken from me all that I had of thee, yet of thy grace leave me the gift which every dog has by nature, that of being true to thee in my distress, when I am deprived of all consolation. This I desire more fervently than thy heavenly kingdom.*[16]

Scripture: Read Psalm 109.

In this psalm, we encounter one of the most furious and vitriolic expressions of anger and hurt imaginable. Scholars are divided about whether in verses 6-20 the speaker is pronouncing a curse upon his enemies or whether the speaker is quoting the curse his enemies have placed upon him as an antidote against it. (The words that the New Revised Standard Version records in verse 6 are not in the Hebrew text, which leaves the identity of the curser ambiguous.) But identifying who is cursing whom is of little import, for even if the speaker is quoting his enemies' curses upon him, he wishes the same curse upon them in return. The imprecation is dire; the curse calls for the extinction of the enemy's memory to the second generation.

Learning the Music

We're not sure we want to learn the music in this psalm. The melody is an angry one. The rage is frightening in its intensity. Yet the speaker's expression of this rage in prayer gives us hope that the psalm contains something of value that we should not overlook. In the psalm's opening verses, the speaker implores God not to be silent when his enemies are attacking him in such unjust fashion. "They . . . attack me without cause. In return for my love they accuse me, even while I make prayer for them." Does this lament sound as though the enemies are strangers or intimates?

Are we more likely to be provoked to this kind of apoplectic rage by strangers or by those close to us? Why?

In the opening verses the speaker implies that he has only been doing what he thought was in the enemies' best interests: He has prayed for them, he has done good to them, and he has shown them love (verses 4-5). How might the speaker have reacted if he had previously treated his enemies with indifference or hostility? Reflect on the times when you have felt absolutely furious at someone—so furious that you lost control or came close to losing control. What caused you to react in such extreme fashion? What might these opening verses tell us about the amount of self-centeredness or ego that may be present in our sense of having been unjustly treated?

Why does the speaker call on God to curse his enemies with such merciless severity? Or to phrase the question differently, why give vent to such furious anger in prayer? What happens to our enemy when we pray our anger? What happens to the pray-er? Who ends up being changed by this vengeful prayer?

In the latter movement of the psalm (verses 22-31), the fury and the speaker appear spent. The speaker casts himself upon God's mercy for vindication, recognizing that while humans may curse, it is God who blesses (verse 28). What does the speaker really want out of all this? Does he want the destruction of his enemies in the terms he has cursed them? Or does he simply want vindication and deliverance? Think again of the time or times when you were so hurt and angry that you felt as violently disposed toward someone as the speaker in this psalm. What did you really want to happen—to you? to the other?

This psalm suggests that it may be safer for us and for our enemies to spend our violent anger in prayer rather than in putting it into action. Before God we cannot hide who we are or the depths of the violence that we harbor inside. To lay it all out before God is to disarm it. Begin to disarm your own inner anger and violence by laying it out before God as fully as you can. This may happen all at once in a great catharsis, or it may be the work of some days or weeks or even months. You may be unaware of the depths within yourself or the focus of the anger you feel. It may be an anger or inner rage you've been harboring for a long time; it may be a fresh provocation. But begin to get in touch with those inner depths out of which violence and vitriol are brought forth; as you feel them welling up, let God see them. Of course, God sees them already; but in the act of letting God see them, healing and conversion begin to happen.

Close your time of prayer today by praying the Lord's Prayer.

Singing the Song

All of us, from time to time, bear the brunt of someone else's deep inner rage and anger. Even when not directed at us, we may find ourselves in an unpleasant or even frightening situation caused by that anger. Begin to notice what kinds of situations seem to bring out that rage. Try to imagine what might have produced hurt so painful that it is expressed in violence, whether the violence is physical or verbal in nature. If the situation is in your family or in your church or in your social circle of friends, begin to pray and seek ways to be a disarming presence. You might offer to be a listening friend or to help the angry person discover alternative ways to unload the outraged feelings.

Preparation

Sit in silence for a few minutes. If thoughts of your day's schedule or events begin to intrude, use a prayer phrase such as those suggested in Day 13 until the intruding thoughts or anxieties are quiet. When you are in a receptive frame of mind and spirit, pray the following prayer by John Henry Newman:

Give me, O my Lord, that purity of conscience which alone can receive your inspirations. My ears are dull, so that I cannot hear your voice. My eyes are dim, so that I cannot see the signs of your presence. You alone can quicken my hearing and purge my sight, and cleanse and renew my heart. Teach me to sit at your feet and to hear your word. Amen.[17]

Scripture: Read Psalm 32.

Psalm 32 is the first of seven penitential psalms that have served for centuries as models for repentance. This first of the seven is in the form of a wisdom psalm, combining a rather didactic beginning and ending that commend and teach the value of repentance. A middle section gives personal testimony to the healing and transforming power of confession and forgiveness. The psalm begins with a double beatitude, "Happy are those whose transgression is forgiven. . . . Happy are those to whom the Lord imputes no iniquity." The personal testimony in the middle (verses 3-7) is at once simple and powerful. First comes the statement about the effects of unconfessed sin, followed by a two-movement drama: "I acknowledged my sin, . . . and you forgave the guilt of my sin." The speaker does not evade responsibility here.

It is important to notice that he does not speak of feeling guilty as modern people often do. We often feel guilty even when we have done nothing wrong. This psalm is not about neurotic feelings of guilt that may accompany poor parenting, childhood failures, or inadequate religious training. The guilt is real; it carries real penalties that detract from bodily health and spiritual well-being. But God's forgiveness is real also and brings a restoration of well-being and health.

Learning the Music

The speaker describes the effects of refusing to acknowledge his wrongdoing: "While I kept silence, my body wasted away through my groaning all day long. . . . My strength was dried up as by the heat of the summer." Think back to a time when you did something that you knew was wrong, something that caused a breach both in your relationship with another person(s) and your relationship with God. What did you do? Did you immediately confess your fault, or did you keep silent and hope that the fault would mend itself?

If you kept silent, how did your silence affect you? Did it make you depressed? irritable with others? sleepless? Did it cause loss of appetite or an eating binge? Spend a few moments examining your own heart. Have you been keeping silent about a wrong you have done to someone? What is the reason for your silence?

The remedy for guilt and its debilitating effects is open confession of the wrongdoing: "Then I acknowledged my sin to you, . . . and you forgave the guilt of my sin." In one sense, this approach may seem a bit simplistic or even a way to avoid responsibility. I wrong another person through my willfulness or malice and I feel bad, so I privately tell God about it and, lo and behold, everything is fine again. I'm forgiven. But is that really the way it works? Where does the person I've wronged enter the equation?

Reflect on your own experiences of wrongdoing, confession, and forgiveness. How did the process work to enable you to experience release from guilt and its effects, which forgiveness entails? What does this suggest to you about the relationships between wrongdoer, the one wronged, and God?

The speaker's assertion, "I acknowledged my sin, . . . you forgave the guilt," is simple but not simplistic. It telescopes the dynamics between wrongdoer, the one wronged, and God into a simple I-Thou confrontation. In the speaker's view, all sin is ultimately sin against God. When we violate our neighbor, we violate our covenant with God. Today it is more fashionable to leave God out of the dynamics of wrongdoing, repression, guilt, the harmful effects, confession, and forgiveness. We view the whole process purely on the human level. Yet the speaker appears to be saying that God is both the one ultimately wronged by our sin, as well as the one who ultimately removes our guilt by forgiveness. In your past instances of wrongdoing, how did you experience that I-Thou encounter with the one to whom you are ultimately accountable? Were you fearful? relieved? embarrassed? Where in your life do you see a need to acknowledge to God your own wrongdoing? What is preventing you from doing that now?

Close your time today by meditating for a few moments on verse 10: "Many are the torments of the wicked, but steadfast love surrounds those who trust in the Lord." Let the reminder of the Lord's steadfast love be a source of strength throughout your day or as you prepare for sleep.

Singing the Song

Begin to notice situations around you—whether in your family, your circle of friends, or in your office or school—where unconfessed wrong is having harmful effects on persons and relationships. As you identify these situations, begin to pray for guidance as to how you could become the catalyst for confession and forgiveness.

Preparation

Use whatever method of centering suits you. If music moves you to prayer, you may want to prepare for the theme of the day by listening to a recording of Gounod's *O Divine Redeemer*, Bizet's *Agnus Dei*, or Andrew Lloyd Webber's *Pie Jesu*, or any music that evokes a penitential mood. The following prayer of a Nigerian Christian may offer you a new image of repentance.

> *God in Heaven, you have helped my life to grow like a tree. Now something has happened. Satan, like a bird, has carried in one twig of his own choosing after another. Before I knew it he had built a dwelling place and was living in it. Tonight, my Father, I am throwing out both the bird and the nest.*[18]

Scripture: Read Psalm 51.

Historically, both Jews and Christians have understood this psalm to be the model for all human confession before God. It is often used liturgically, and traditionally this psalm introduces the season of Lent. It is cast in the form of an individual's personal confession; the title says, "A Psalm of David, when the prophet Nathan came to him, after he had gone in to Bathsheba." Probably the psalm is a devout meditation upon the story of David's violation of Bathsheba and his murder of her husband Uriah, which was written several centuries later for use in public worship.

Sharing language and concepts with the books of Isaiah and Ezekiel, it appears to have been generated sometime after the Exile in prophetic circles. The structure and movement of the psalm is clear. Verses 1-2 are a plea for God's mercy. The confession proper comes in verses 3-5, followed by an acknowledgment of God's just demand for righteousness and a plea for a transformed heart (verses 6-12). Verses 13-17 promise amendment of life, exemplary behavior, and the praise of God for the gift of forgiveness and restoration. Verses 18-19 may well have been added later to emphasize that verses 16-17 were not a polemic against all sacrifices—only those unaccompanied by the proper spirit of penitence.

Learning the Music

The psalm begins with a plea for God to be gracious: "Have mercy on me, O God." The psalmist's language (stating the request three times) lends intensity to the plea:

> Blot out my transgressions.
> Wash me thoroughly from my iniquity,
> and cleanse me from my sin.

Why do you think the speaker begins by throwing himself on the mercy of the court, so to speak? Why does he not begin by introducing a mitigating circumstance, presenting himself in the best light possible, or asking to be judged on his merits as well as his demerits before getting into the matter of confession?

Look at the confession itself in verses 3-5. He doesn't beat around the bush or attempt to evade responsibility, put the best light possible on the wrong being confessed, or blame any-one or anything else. Reflect on your own approach to God when you feel that something has breached your relationship with God. Are your own confessions this honest or do you flavor them with attempts at self-justification? "Lord, I know that what I did was wrong, but . . ."

The speaker says, "Against you, you alone, have I sinned." Does this imply that no human being has been injured by the speaker's sin, that God is the exclusive and sole injured party? It may help your reflection to read this as it has traditionally been read as David's confession following his adultery with Bathsheba and his murder of Uriah. Read a narrative account of David's acknowledgment of his guilt in the matter in 2 Samuel 12. When does an act become a sin rather than a mistake in judgment, the result of a neurosis, or inappropriate behavior resulting from weakness or ignorance?

What (and whose!) criteria determine whether an act is a sin? How does the confession, "I lied to Sally" become "I have sinned against God"? Use your own personal experience to help you shape your thinking about the relationship between our acts, their effects on other people, and our relationship with God. What has made you aware that some of your actions have been sinful rather than simply unfortunate?

Part of the psalmist's confession involves acknowledging his complete culpability: "Indeed I was born guilty, a sinner when my mother conceived me." Sometimes people have used this statement to support the doctrine of original sin—that we are born sinners. More likely, this verse is a deeply personal, if hyperbolic, expression of consciousness of being in the wrong in relationship to God. It is a person confessing who he is before God; he is a sinner, or violator of God's will and law, through and through. Why is such ruthless self-evaluation a necessary part of repentance? Or, to put it another way, why is acceptance of ourselves as sinners a necessary corollary of our hope for forgiveness and inner transformation? Can you trust God enough to confess who you are in the deepest and darkest parts of your own being?

The speaker's prayer links a clean heart and a new and right spirit with the restoration of the gift of God's spirit and the return of joy in God's saving love. Why are the two necessarily connected? If a clean heart, resulting from honest confession, implies the restoration of God's presence (Spirit), what does unconfessed sin imply about our failure to experience God's presence in our lives? Where in your life do you see that same connection?

Honest confession of sin, arising out of genuine sorrow or contrition, brings results beyond the restoration of the sinner to right relationship with God (verses 13-15). Inward transformation has outward and visible effects: the public praise of God and a desire to reach out to other sinners. In other words, just as sin moves beyond being a private matter to impact the community, so the transformation of the sinner by God's forgiving grace has a public dimension. Why is this, and where do you see this connection in your own life and experience?

Close your time today by slowly praying this psalm all the way through, making it your own as far as you are able. Apply it specifically to the sins that honest self-examination have revealed in your own life.

Singing the Song

Among your circle of family, friends, and acquaintances, where can you identify breaches in relationship that honest confession and mutual forgiveness could heal? With no sense of superiority, where might you be the agent of that healing because of what you have learned in your own experience?

Group Session

Gathering

Several of the psalms for this week have found their way into the hymnbooks, particularly Psalms 51 and 137. One hymn common to many hymnals is "O for a Closer Walk with God" by William Cowper. The hymn is a meditation on Psalm 51:12 and expresses many of themes raised this week. Your group may want to sing it together as a way to open the session. In the musical *Godspell*, one song from that musical, "On the Willows," is a haunting rendition of Psalm 137. If someone in the group has a recording, you may want to listen to that song together.

Discussion

Remember to be selective as you look at the questions below. Don't feel you have to address each question in your group discussion.

1. Psalm 55 raised the issue of the correspondence between a deep, personal hurt and the perception of a general moral decline or the feeling that everyone is against me (us). Where in the world around you do you see evidence of the same pattern? How does this insight illuminate (though not fully explain) some of the conflicts between nations or ethnic groups?

2. The experience of the exiles in Babylon, unable to sing the Lord's song in an alien setting and bound by their memories of Zion, is a common one—not only on the personal level but in larger terms as well. Where do you see evidence in your church or in your city or even in the country as a whole of this longing for a remembered golden age of the past that is blocking the ability to see God at work in the present? Warning: This subject could lend itself to a discussion of partisan politics. Resist the temptation to allow this to happen. No particular viewpoint on the political spectrum is representative of either the problem or the solution. Keep the discussion on the level of how individuals and communities feel, and how those feelings are made visible in particular circumstances.

3. How does one sing the Lord's song in an alien land? If the Christian community is always a community that is "pilgrim through this barren land," as the hymn "Guide Me, O Thou Great Jehovah" puts it, how can we sing the songs of Zion in the midst of Babylon without either withdrawing into ourselves or surrendering completely to the culture that surrounds us?

4. In recent years, those within religious circles have tended to downplay the categories of right and wrong in human behavior, and with them the attendant categories of guilt and forgiveness. We often label behavior appropriate or inappropriate and explain it in psychological or social categories rather than in moral ones. People act badly because they have low self-esteem or because they feel powerless and need to assert themselves.

Yet other voices speak. In *Whatever Became of Sin?* eminent psychiatrist Karl Menninger argued that the recovery of moral categories in discourse about human behavior is fundamental to mental and spiritual health. However as society becomes more culturally and religiously diverse, it has less basis for consensus about what the moral categories of right and wrong, good and evil, sin and sanctity are.

What is the value (or lack of value) in continuing to use words like *sin*, *guilt*, *repentance*, *forgiveness*, and *grace*? Does such language have any meaning outside of its use in liturgy? Does it have meaning only for individual persons who belong to a community that shares a common understanding of those categories? In what ways might it be meaningful in the larger society?

Abraham Lincoln declared a Day of National Repentance following the Civil War. Could such a day have meaning now in our religiously pluralistic society? What would such repentance look like on a personal level? on a national level? (These questions have vast implications. You may want to focus in on just one aspect in order to avoid getting lost in a general free-for-all.)

5. How did your reflection on Psalm 109 affect you? What were your reactions to the violent curses called down upon the speaker's enemy? What value, if any, do you see in allowing the rage expressed in that curse to be given voice in prayer?

6. What happens when we forgive someone who has wronged us? Do we exact a penalty or do we let them off the hook? What are the implications of forgiveness for the one who committed the wrong? for the one who was wronged? Do we forgive and forget? What new possibilities does repentance and forgiveness open up?

Closing

Pray Psalm 51 aloud together as a way to close the session. You may want to join hands in a circle as a way of expressing your solidarity with one another as forgiven sinners.

Week Four

DURING

Psalms of Waiting

dur·ing *prep.* **1.** Throughout the course or duration of. **2.** At some time in.

My tears have been my food day and night,
while people say to me continually,
"Where is your God?"

—Psalm 42:3

THIS WEEK'S PREPOSITION THAT CHARACTERIZES the spiritual movement has the shortest definition and the longest actual experience of any of the movements of our lives. Waiting is perhaps the most common experience of life. Moments of action punctuate long stretches of waiting. Just as we may read, type, or play computer games while being kept on hold on the telephone, so we may be actively engaged in one area of life, while in other areas we are still waiting.

While waiting may be life's most common experience, not all waiting is alike. What we are waiting for will, to a large extent, determine how we experience the wait. A condemned prisoner awaiting execution at dawn and a child on Christmas Eve awaiting the minutes until she can wake up her sleeping parents and begin opening her Christmas presents are both waiting—yet the waiting for each is vastly different. An elderly woman living out her days in a nursing home, her body no longer under her own control, and her mind only episodically lucid is waiting, as is the young couple anticipating the onset of labor that will herald the birth of their first child. The one waits in weary resignation; the other waits in joyous expectation.

The common element in all waiting is the sense that time drags slowly. It is *during* the action that time flies. Whether one is waiting actively in hope or fear, or passively in resignation or boredom, time seems to slow down. The end, whether it is anticipated with joy or foreboding, seems like it will never come. In action, time is compressed; in waiting, time expands.

Both meanings of the word *during* describe particular aspects of the experience of waiting. The first describes the sense of continuation that is common to waiting. Time goes on. The present moment appears to have no predecessor or successor; it elongates, stretches out, continues. Nothing seems to be happening. The second definition describes the sense of individual moments or points during the waiting when something happens. It may not be a moment of action but a moment of clarity, a moment of revelation, when we feel that something is happening even in the midst of the waiting. Time is not only expanding in duration but is taking on a particular texture or feel.

THE PSALMS FOR THIS WEEK will express both dimensions of the experience of waiting. In comparison with the other three movements we have already studied, *during* is a quieter movement. The activity and sometimes headlong pace of *up* is missing. Gone too are the devastation and fear that life is caving in on us. The sense of struggle and the pain of growth as we try to cope with the crisis that has plunged us into the depths has given way to something else. We are still *down*, but we are not still falling.

We have bottomed out, as it were; and while we still want to go back *up*, we've learned that life exists here on the bottom as well. Our downward plunge did not make an end of us; in fact, it may have brought us to a new beginning. But there is still more to be learned down here on the bottom side of life. We're waiting to discover what it is.

Sometimes the waiting is hard, because we still have a great deal of fear. We don't know what the outcome will be, and we're not really certain it will be good. But in moments of lucid clarity, we catch a fleeting glimpse or hear a word spoken into our silence that kindles our hope. Expectation begins to color our waiting. Something has ended, but we are still alive. Something has begun, but we don't know where it will lead. Fear and hope intermingle. So we wait—sometimes impatiently, plaintively asking as time stretches out, "How long, O Lord? Will you forget me forever?" At other times, expectation fills us; we can hardly wait, as the common expression puts it. "My soul waits for the Lord more than those who wait for the morning." But whether we wait in fear or hope, patience or frustration, if we pay attention, we discover that God is present in this time of waiting; in fact, God waits with us and for us.

Preparation

As you come to your time of prayer today, reflect on this prayer of Saint Thérèse of Liseaux as a possible model for waiting in faith and hope.

> *Just for today,*
> *what does it matter, O Lord, if the future is dark?*
> *To pray now for tomorrow I am not able.*
> *Keep my heart only for today,*
> *grant me your light —*
> *just for today.*[19]

Scripture: Read Psalm 25.

The structure of this psalm is that of an acrostic: Each verse begins with the succeeding letter of the Hebrew alphabet. While this structure places constraints to some degree on the psalm's content, the author has managed to make it thematically coherent. It is predominantly a prayer for individual help, though the acrostic structure and the emphasis on teaching (verses 4, 8-9, 12) make it appear that the purpose of the psalm is to teach people how to pray for God's help. The theme of waiting for God to act in the midst of one's troubles recurs in verses 3, 5, and 21.

Learning the Music

The opening verses of the psalm establish the speaker's feelings of helplessness in controlling his own life and his sense of utter dependence upon God. The phrases *To you, O Lord, I lift up my soul; O my God, in you I trust;* and *Do not let those who wait for you be put to shame* convey the attitude of someone who knows that he has no recourse for help or vindication except in God. When have you felt similarly helpless? When have you felt that you simply did not have the resources within yourself or at your command to deal with your situation? Did you, like the psalmist, feel that you were totally dependent upon God at that point or did that sense of positive dependence not enter your perception of the situation? Does the perception that we are totally dependent upon God make the waiting times easier or harder?

The speaker asks God to remember something and forget something. He asks God not only to remember the steadfast love and mercy God has showed to others but to show it to him as well. He also asks God to forget his sins, not in the sense of overlooking them but in the sense of pardoning his guilt (verse 11), so that his sins are not a factor in God's willingness to rescue him from his predicament. We are more familiar with, and perhaps more comfortable with, the notion of asking God to forgive us than we are with the notion of asking God to remember God's own steadfast love and mercy in the past. Does the psalmist fear that God will forget how to act? What do you make of this request, and do you view it as an appropriate or inappropriate way to address God in prayer? What human feelings and concerns does the psalmist raise?

After affirming that God will guide those who fear the Lord (verses 11-15), the psalm ends with a renewed plea for God to relieve the distress of the speaker and a reiteration of the fact that the speaker is waiting for God to act (verse 21). In your own times of waiting for a problematic or painful situation to change, are you as persistent as this psalmist in pressing your case with God? Why should persistence in prayer for God's help be necessary in any sense? What value, if any, can you see in such persistence during a time of painful waiting?

Close your time today by praying the psalm through from beginning to end. Let it resonate with your own experience of waiting for relief or light to come into your darkness.

Singing the Song

Who among your circle of close friends or family members is on hold in the midst of a difficult or painful situation? In what ways might you can enter that waiting with them, giving them the hope that God has not forgotten them?

Day 17

Preparation

Use whatever method you find most useful and comfortable to center your inner focus on God. Then meditate for a few moments on this prayer by Saint Ignatius of Loyola:

> *Take, Lord, all my liberty. Receive my memory, my understanding and my whole will. Whatever I have and possess thou hast given to me; to thee I restore it wholly, and to thy will I utterly surrender it for thy direction. Give me the love of thee only, with thy grace, and I am rich enough; nor ask I anything beside.*[20]

Scripture: Read Psalms 42–43.

Psalms 42 and 43 are really only one psalm. Psalm 43 has no separate title, and the language and thought continues from Psalm 42. We do not know why the editors and compilers of the psalter separated them. It is one of the most beautiful of the individual laments, though both content and structure indicate that it is designed for liturgical use. The refrain, which occurs in 42:5-6, 11; 43:5, provides the structure for the psalm: Each recurrence marks the end of a plaintive lament.

The spiritual state of the speaker fits that state the classic writings on the spiritual life often describe as "the dark night" of the soul. Many sincere Christians have discovered times, sometimes relatively short and sometimes of long duration, when their sense of God's nearness or presence disappears. Occasionally they can trace the reason to a specific event or set of circumstances, to a broken relationship, to bodily illness, or life-stage changes. However at other times, they cannot pinpoint the cause of the dark night. One still believes and lives faithfully during these times, but a numbness or a darkness exists where the reality of God's presence used to be.

Learning the Music

To one who has known the strong and comforting presence of God and who now feels that God is absent, the intense longing in the opening verses of this psalm may strike a resonant chord. The imagery of a desperate thirst for water, which is an essential element of life, is balanced by an ironic statement that the only water available is the speaker's own tears. Have you ever known such an intense longing for God's presence? You may be experiencing such a time of spiritual darkness now. Describe that experience, whether present or past, when

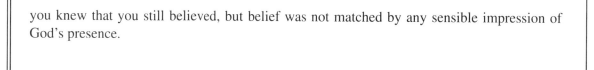

you knew that you still believed, but belief was not matched by any sensible impression of God's presence.

The anguish of God's absence is answered by remembrance. In 42:4, the speaker remembers having praised God joyfully in the midst of the worshiping congregation. In other words, the speaker contrasts his feelings of isolation and alienation with his memories of God's closeness during corporate worship. This remembrance leads to the first instance of the refrain, "Why are you cast down, O my soul, and why are you disquieted within me? Hope in God; for I shall again praise him, my help and my God." Reflect on a time when you felt that God was absent and your memories of former times when you felt God's closeness helped rekindle your hope. You may be going through such a time now. If you are, spend these moments remembering when it was and under what circumstances you felt God's closeness. What was different or distinctive about that time?

The speaker attaches his memories of a former sense of God's presence to his memories of worship within the community of faith. For a few moments explore the connections in your own life between community and personal awareness of God's presence. Often when tragedy or deep disappointment come to us, our first reaction is to absent ourselves from public worship. We don't feel like talking to anyone, and we don't want others to talk to us about whatever has overtaken us. What might this psalm have to say about the wisdom or folly of that reaction?

After the rekindling of hope through remembrance of participation within the community of praise, the speaker returns to his lament: "My soul is cast down within me." Immediately, however, memory comes to his rescue again—this time with a more personal remembrance. This time he remembers not the praise of God in the public worship but God's presence: "I remember you from the land of Jordan and of Hermon, from Mount Mizar." Once again God is an assured reality to the speaker, but this makes his dilemma even more painful. If God really is present, why is the speaker still languishing in the dark? "I say to God my rock, 'Why have you forgotten me?'" The speaker responds to his own question in 42:11 with the second statement of the refrain: "Hope in God; for I shall again praise him, my help and my God." How is the refrain an answer (or not an answer) to the question of God's having forgotten him? What does it mean to hope in God? to affirm God as my help? What help?

At the beginning of Psalm 43, the prayer changes tone from tearful lament and petulant questioning to passionate petition: "Vindicate me, O God. . . . O send out your light and your truth." This petition is accompanied by a positive affirmation of the speaker's relationship to God: "You are the God in whom I take refuge" and a resolve to once again praise God among the faithful community when God acts on his petition and rescues him. The psalm then ends with a final refrain, "Hope in God; for I shall again praise him, my help and my God." Thinking again of your own experiences of spiritual darkness, which of the elements in this psalm (plaintive lament, whining or angry questioning, memory of God's presence experienced in and through the praise of God in community with other faithful people, a positive affirmation of trust) were present or lacking in your own dark night of the soul? What do these elements contribute to the ability to wait in hope rather than waiting in despair?

Close your time by praying through the psalm again, letting the refrain sink deeply into your heart and mind.

Singing the Song

Our individualistic culture and religious traditions often tempt us to think that our spiritual well-being is a private matter, that we should be able to dig our way out of spiritual dark holes on our own. Perhaps it's time to rethink the place of community in your own life, particularly a faith community. Begin to formulate some plan to deepen your own experience of praising God from among a faithful community, either through becoming more deeply involved in your church and its worship or perhaps by seeking out other persons with whom you can share your respective journeys and become a hope-filled community for one another.

If you are a regular participant in a faith community, you may want to be alert to others within that community who are going through difficult times and who appear to be dropping out or absenting themselves from the community because of depression or loss or some crisis. Without being pushy, try to discover a way to reach out to those persons and help them to remember God's presence as they experienced it in community.

Preparation

To center yourself and to adopt a listening inner disposition, breathe deeply and rhythmically for a few moments using the name of Jesus. Silently breathe the first syllable as you inhale and the second syllable as you exhale. When you feel a sense of inner quiet, read and meditate on the following prayer by Saint Clement of Rome:

> *We beseech you, O God, to be our help and succor. Save those who are in tribulation; have mercy on the lonely; lift up the fallen; show yourself to the needy; heal the ungodly; convert the wanderers of your people; feed the hungry; raise up the weak; comfort the fainthearted. Let all the peoples know that you are God alone, and Jesus Christ is your Son, and we are your people and the sheep of your pasture; for the sake of Christ Jesus. Amen.[21]*

Scripture: Read Psalm 13.

The shortest of the personal laments in the psalter, this psalm has often been seen as a model prayer for help. The structure is simple but significant. The psalm begins with the complaint, "How long, O Lord? Will you forget me forever?" The speaker then repeats the words *how long* four times for emphasis in a quadruple parallelism. The petition follows the lament in verses 3-4. It states the harm that will come to the speaker if God does not answer. Finally the tone of long-suffering and urgent need give way to a statement of trust in the Lord, which is stated in the past rather than the future: "I trusted in your steadfast love. . . . [the Lord] has dealt bountifully with me."

Learning the Music

The four repetitions of the lament, "How long, O Lord?" are a powerful statement of the experience of *during*. The feeling that God has abandoned us and left us to stew in our own juices is common to those who are waiting for life to get better than it is. Perhaps the crisis is past, perhaps the painful struggle to grow in the face of the crisis is past also. Yet nothing good is happening, at least nothing that we can identify. Like the speaker, we still have pain in our souls, and we still feel God's face is turned away from us. Why do we feel that way? Why does waiting feel like abandonment?

The speaker's petition, "Give light to my eyes, or I will sleep the sleep of death" is similar to our expression, "If something doesn't happen soon, I'm going to just die." Actual death is probably not a real possibility here; this is the hyperbole of someone who feels extremely frustrated and whose patience is almost exhausted waiting for things to change. When in your life have you felt that complete sense of frustration with a status quo that seemed like it would go on forever? Why were you so frustrated?

The speaker fears that if things do not change soon, his enemies will gloat. In your own experiences of frustrated waiting, how much of your frustration was bound up with your fear of what other people would think about you? How would freedom from that fear make a difference in the waiting?

In the midst of this expression of frustration, hope breaks in. The speaker affirms his trust in God, and his intention to rejoice in God's salvation. What is the relationship between frustration and hope? How do the two connect and intertwine in prayer?

What significance do you see in the speaker's unusual way of using the past tense instead of the present or the future to express his hope in the midst of frustration? It would be more normal to say "I trust in the Lord" or "I believe that the Lord will deal bountifully with me." What dynamic is going on here, and what light does it offer you for understanding your own experiences of frustrated waiting?

Close your prayer today by praying the whole psalm through again, allowing it to provide you with a bridge from your own frustration and impatience to hopeful trust.

Singing the Song

If you are aware of someone in your family or at your workplace or among your friends whose life is on hold, and who appears frustrated and impatient, see if you can identify the root of his or her frustration. Don't play amateur psychologist but be a compassionate observer. Then try to imagine a way in which you could become an agent of hope, either through sharing your own experiences of frustrated waiting in hope or simply by praying with him or her, perhaps even using this psalm.

Day 19

Preparation

Use the following prayer of Thomas à Kempis, author of the classic *Of the Imitation of Christ* to lead you into your reflection today:

> *Write your blessed name, O Lord, upon my heart, there to remain so indelibly engraven, that no prosperity, no adversity, shall ever move me from your love. Be to me a strong tower of defense, a comforter in tribulation, a deliverer in distress, a very present help in trouble, and a guide to heaven through the many temptations and dangers of this life. Amen.*[22]

Scripture: Read Psalm 130.

Despite its brevity, this short psalm has influenced the history of liturgy and spirituality greatly. It serves as the basis of the ancient liturgical canticle "De Profundis," which has been set to song in hymns, anthems, and chants. Martin Luther's hymn text and tune, arranged by Bach, is probably the most familiar and is found in most hymnals. Walter Brueggemann refers to it as the miserable cry of a nobody from nowhere, who nevertheless penetrates the veil of heaven! It is heard and received. While considered one of the seven penitential psalms, it is marked by a particularly strong note of hope.

Learning the Music

The psalm begins with a cry from the depths. In modern slang, we might be refer to this experience as life in "the pits." We all know what life is like in the pits, because we all have spent time there. And while we are there, a cry for help is about all the prayer we can muster. Helplessness and the sense of being utterly without resources of our own or even the resources of others characterizes life in the depths.

Verses 3-4 embody a profound theology that may help us understand the influence of this psalm on the history of spirituality. Verse 3 gives voice to a common feeling of one who is in the depths; it expresses the fear that we are in the bottom of the hole because of some sin or offense we've committed. Get in touch with your own experiences in the pits, whether in the past or current experience. Was (or is) there an element of fear present?

Was (is) the fear related to the concern of having offended God in some way, and how did that fear contribute to your sense of helplessness? To what do you trace the source of that fear?

Why do we imagine that God is a God whose principal activity is to mark iniquities? One of the most famous expressions of that image of God is the sermon preached by Jonathan Edwards in eighteenth-century New England, "Sinners in the Hands of an Angry God." In it, Edwards likened his audience to loathsome spiders whom God was holding suspended over the flames of hell, ready to destroy them because of their foul sins. Accounts of the occasion tell us that people in the congregation fainted in terror.

Though the speaker in the psalm is crying out from the depths, he decisively demolishes that image of God. In verse 4 he says, "But there is forgiveness with you, so that you may be revered." What is the significance of the order of things expressed in that affirmation? Does the experience of forgiveness result in reverence for God or is reverence for God a condition of forgiveness? By which order has your own relationship to God been governed?

The speaker gives voice to a deep longing for a restoration of a sense of God's presence and the deliverance that he hopes God will bring. What is the relationship between our image of God and our ability to endure "the pits" in hope? What is your prevailing image of God? What connection do you see between that image and your own ability, or lack of it, to live in hope?

The psalm concludes with a fervent exhortation to the whole community to live in hope because it is the Lord's nature to show steadfast love and great power to redeem. The hope expressed here is not just wishful thinking; it has moved beyond longing to anticipation and settled trust that God will act to deliver, not only the speaker, but all Israel from the depths. How do you see that move from wistful hopefulness to firm confidence that God will deliver you taking place in your own situation? What in your faith as it currently exists is capable of producing and sustaining such a shift? Where may you need to enlarge or change your faith?

Close your time by meditating on verses 7-8 and give thanks for the Lord's steadfast love that is with us even when we are crying out from the depths.

Singing the Song

Begin to notice the images of God that others express or implying as they speak of their own experiences. Become aware of those images in the church school material that your church uses; in the religious programs on radio and television that you listen to or watching; or, by reflection, on what your parents or family members taught you. In what ways do those images lend themselves to the growth of hope within people who are in the depths? Begin to consider ways you can help others overcome those negative images of God.

Preparation

Use the Jesus Prayer (*Lord Jesus Christ, Son of God, have mercy on me*) or another prayer phrase of your own choosing. Repeat the prayer silently or aloud, in rhythm with your breathing for several minutes until you are centered inwardly. You may choose to reflect on this prayer to Christ by Saint Ambrose of Milan, the spiritual mentor and teacher of Augustine.

> *You are medicine for me when I am sick. You are my strength when I need help. You are life itself when I fear death. You are the way when I long for heaven. You are light when all is dark. You are my food when I need nourishment.*[23]

Scripture: Read Psalm 63.

The setting imagined for this psalm and expressed in its title was the experience of David in the wilderness of Judah (or Judea), to which he had fled from the murderous political jealousy of King Saul. For David, that desert was both a place of refuge and of exile. The psalm is at once a personal plea for help and an affirmation of faith. The speaker counters the barren experience of waiting expressed in the first verse with the remembrance in verse 2 of God's presence and steadfast love, which he discovered and experienced in the sanctuary (in corporate worship). This remembrance satisfies the longing of the person waiting.

Learning the Music

The waiting experience described here is not that of someone who doubts whether God exists or cares but rather the waiting of someone who can begin a prayer for help with a firm confession: "O God, you are my God, I seek you." The speaker expresses his longing for God in vivid imagery: "My soul thirsts for you; my flesh faints for you, as in a dry and weary land where there is no water." When have you experienced a similarly intense longing for God during a time of spiritual or emotional dryness? Was your longing tinged with doubt about God's love or goodness, or were you convinced of that love and goodness even though you were not presently experiencing it?

How does a conviction of God's steadfast love make a difference in the experience of waiting?

The speaker's conviction that God's steadfast love is a reality even though currently he cannot feel it, finds its roots in his past experience of having glimpsed God's power and glory through the worship and praise of God among the community of faith. In the experience of praising God in company with other worshipers, he has become convinced of God's steadfast love, which is better than life. This conviction evokes a response of continued praise even in the midst of this dry and weary land. What does this suggest about the importance of worship in community? What place has corporate worship played in your own life and in your sense of God's presence even during a barren experience of waiting? What relationship is there, if any, between the faith of each individual and the faith of the community as a whole? When I am experiencing a time of spiritual barrenness or alienation, what difference does it make to myself or my faith community if I am present in worship or not?

For the speaker, the memory of God's steadfast love glimpsed in previous experiences of worship, rekindles his own conviction that God is present even in the wilderness. This conviction sustains him during the waiting and uncertainty (verses 5-8). He relaxes rather than frets. Yet his situation is still unresolved. He is still waiting, and the outcome of his waiting is still uncertain. Yet he experiences that uncertainty as hope rather than despair: "My

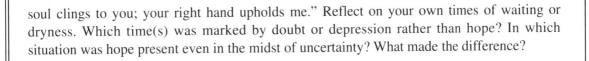

soul clings to you; your right hand upholds me." Reflect on your own times of waiting or dryness. Which time(s) was marked by doubt or depression rather than hope? In which situation was hope present even in the midst of uncertainty? What made the difference?

The speaker's experience of recalling God's power and glory experienced in the sanctuary and his subsequent ability to relax and wait in hope, causes him to express his confidence that his enemies will not win out in the end. In the end, they will be defeated and he will be vindicated. What is the relationship between hope and confidence? How do you see that relationship at work in your own life? Or where is that relationship missing in your life?

Close your time by praying this psalm through again. As far as you are able, let it give voice to your own deepest needs and desires.

Singing the Song

Our individualistic culture often prevents us from knowing the strength and resources we can derive from community. As you participate in worship in your church, begin to intentionally pay attention to what is going on when people praise God in community. If you become aware of persons in your church whose lives are on hold and who appear to be going through a spiritually dry period of waiting, try to think of ways you might trigger the remembrance of God's power and glory, which will sustain them and offer them hope in the midst of their desert experience. It may be a word of encouragement, an offer to be a sympathetic listener, a promise to pray for them daily, or a call to say that you've missed them in church if they have been absent.

Group Session

Gathering

Many hymnals contain settings of this week's psalms. You may want to begin your time together by singing one from your church's hymnal. You may want to read one of the day's psalms aloud together, perhaps either Psalms 42–43 or Psalm 63.

Discussion

You may choose to discuss one or two of the questions below for the whole time or spend a briefer time and try to give attention to several of them.

1. Spend some time discussing how the movement for this week *during* differs from or relates to *down* or *through*.

2. Why is waiting so difficult for most of us? Why do doubt, frustration, or even numb hopelessness frequently characterize our experiences of waiting?

3. One or two group members may be willing to describe a time of spiritual dryness or barren waiting in their own lives. They would simply describe the experience: what it felt like; what fears, doubts, questions it raised; and what resources they discovered for learning to wait in hope.

4. Which psalm this week captured the experience of waiting most accurately and powerfully for you? Which one offered you a new insight and helped you understand your own life more clearly or helped you grow in your knowledge of God's ways with you?

5. Psalm 63 strongly connected community worship and the personal ability to trust and hope during a desert experience. Discuss that connection: Why go to church? or What is the truth or fallacy in the expression that one can worship God through contemplation of nature (a walk on the beach or through the woods) as one can in church?

Closing

Spend a few moments in silence together, centering yourself and also tuning in to the others in the group. Then pray Psalm 130 aloud together.

FROM

Psalms of Deliverance

from *prep.* **fr. 1.a.** Used to indicate a specified place or time as a starting point. **2.** Used to indicate a source, a cause, an agent, or an instrument. **3.** Used to indicate separation, removal, or exclusion. **5.** Because of.

> *You are a hiding place for me;*
> *you preserve me from trouble;*
> *you surround me with glad cries*
> *of deliverance.*
> —Psalm 32:7

A PASSER-BY, HEARING THE CRIES OF A CHILD who has fallen into a steep-sided ditch, rescues her. Deliverance! The jury acquits the man falsely accused and put on trial for his life. Deliverance! The depressed woman who has grieved her husband's untimely death for many months suddenly notices the sunshine, and life begins to seem good again. Deliverance! The adults permit the boy to play outside instead of having to linger at the table listening to boring adult conversation. Deliverance!

Deliverance comes in many forms, but the feeling it produces is similar in each—a sense of having been rescued, of emerging alive from great peril or deadly depression. Relief mingles with surprise and joy. The downward plunge into crisis; the painful and often slow awakening of self-knowledge and struggle to grow; the long, seemingly endless waiting for circumstances or ourselves or other people to change become but a memory in the rush of joy and well-being that floods in when life begins to climb upward again. Colors are more intense, odors are more pungent, sounds are clearer and more melodious. We're alive and life is worth living!

The psalms give voice to several aspects of the experience of deliverance. One is the feeling of exhilaration and relief itself. However, along with that feeling we often hear God praised as the source of deliverance *from* death, *from* fear, *from* enemies, *from* false accusation, and *from* troubles, to name only a few. Another aspect is the contrast between what was and what is now. Just as the laments contrasted the good times of former days with the bad times of current days, so the psalms of deliverance contrast the unhappiness and anguish of the past with the heady joy of the present moment. Life is headed up again, promising to get even better. We are not yet back on an even keel, but we're getting there. There has been a turnaround. We've been delivered! A verse from one of Charles Wesley's hymns expresses the mood of this week's psalms well:

> *Long my imprisoned spirit lay,*
> *fast bound in sin and nature's night;*
> *thine eye diffused a quickening ray;*
> *I woke, the dungeon flamed with light;*
> *my chains fell off, my heart was free,*
> *I rose, went forth, and followed thee.*

Preparation

To prepare yourself for prayer, you may want to listen to a particular piece of music that carries you into a contemplative or celebrative mood. Or you may prefer a time of silence, using rhythmical breathing and a prayer phrase such as the Jesus Prayer to draw you inward. The following prayer by Saint Anselm of Canterbury expresses the spirit of thanksgiving and rejoicing in God's saving love that will mark this week's psalms:

O God, You are Life, Wisdom, Truth, Bounty, and Blessedness, the Eternal, the only true Good! My God and my Lord, You are my hope and my heart's joy. I confess, with thanksgiving, that You have made me in your image, that I may direct all my thoughts to You, and love You. O God, make me to know You aright, that I may more and more love, and enjoy, and possess You. And since, in the life here below, I cannot fully attain this blessedness, let it at least grow in me day by day, until it all be fulfilled at last in the life to come. Here be the knowledge of You increased, and there let it be perfected. Here let my love to You grow and there let it ripen; that my joy being here great in hope, may there in fruition be made perfect. Amen.[24]

Scripture: Read Psalm 9.

Psalms 9 and 10 are really one psalm, though most English translations of the Bible assign them separate numbers. However, in Hebrew it is clear that they are a single composition because the structure is that of an acrostic: Each poetic verse begins with a succeeding letter of the Hebrew alphabet. Because both psalms are lengthy and because Psalm 10 is in the form of a lament rather than a song of deliverance, we will only deal with the part designated Psalm 9. You may wish to read the two together to get a sense of the whole.

Because of the acrostic structure, the organization of the psalm can appear confusing—various themes interweave with one another rather than presenting themselves in an orderly fashion. One key point to note is that the psalmist has personified the community of Israel as an individual. So the opposing forces in the psalm are "me" and "the nations" (Gentiles), with the "me" standing for the community of God's people and "the nations" standing for the enemies who are oppressing the faithful community. This personification of the community as an individual marks this psalm as a piece of community liturgy used after national deliverance from powerful enemies.

Learning the Music

The psalm begins with thanksgiving to God for deliverance from enemies. Unlike expressions of thanksgiving found in some of the psalms in the first week's study, this one does not attribute deliverance to the superior righteousness of the speaker (or the community) nor to the speaker or community's superior strength of arms. The speaker in Psalm 9 clearly recognizes that the deliverance is God's doing: "I will tell of all your wonderful deeds. . . . When my enemies turned back, they stumbled and perished before you." When have you experienced a deliverance from some oppressive or painful situation that you could attribute only to God's act and not your own strength or a lucky chance? How did you respond to that deliverance?

The defeat of the enemies is total: "The enemies have vanished in everlasting ruins; . . . the very memory of them has perished." Often when we experience deliverance from enemies (feel free to interpret *enemies* in the broadest sense of any oppressive or defeating circumstance or situation), we have difficulty forgetting the power of the enemies. The memory of our defeat lingers long after the power of what has been defeating us has been broken. Reflecting on your own experience, when have you known the lingering memory of your oppression or painful experience that has caused your deliverance to be less than complete or that occasionally has plunged you back down into defeat? What does this tell you about the power of memories to shape our present experience?

The psalm suggests that an antidote to our lingering memories of the enemy is the remembrance of God's power and the recital of God's deeds: "I will tell of all your wonderful deeds. . . . The Lord sits enthroned forever. . . . The Lord is a stronghold for the oppressed. . . . For you, O Lord, have not forsaken those who seek you. . . . Sing praises to the Lord, . . . declare his deeds among the peoples." What is the relationship between recital of God's deeds and the experience of deliverance? Use your own experience as the touchstone here. Where do you see that connection or lack of it in your own life? How might the memory of God's deeds rather than the memory of the enemy's deeds make a difference in your own life?

This psalm repeatedly names God as the one who is on the side of the oppressed and needy (verses 9, 12, 18). However, when we are in the black hole of defeat or despair, this truth—if it is a truth—is not always obvious or apparent. When we're down, it doesn't feel as though God is on our side. It is only when deliverance comes that we perceive God's hand in our situation in retrospect. In your own experience, what connections do you make between hindsight and faith, between past experiences of God's faithfulness and your ability to trust God and affirm God's care for you in the present?

Close your time of prayer today by meditating for some moments on verses 9-10. You may want to repeat them aloud several times, allowing them to sink into your soul.

Singing the Song

Who among your family members or friendship circles needs to experience deliverance? Begin to reflect on their situation and see if there is a way in which you can become the remembrance of God to them, a living reminder that God is a stronghold in times of trouble—for them. Don't preach at them or lecture them, but try to discover ways in which you can help them move beyond their memories of the enemies by remembering God's saving deeds in the past.

Preparation

The use of candles to represent our prayers is an ancient Christian practice. Votive candles dating back to at least the second century have been discovered in the ruins of an older church beneath John Calvin's cathedral in Geneva. You may wish to use a candle or candles for a few days to see if this ancient practice has meaning for you today. Place one or more candles on a table near the place where you normally pray. Think of a need or a person for whom you wish to pray. It may be a personal need of your own or someone else's need for whom you wish to intercede. Light the candles, one for each request or petition, as you voice them either aloud or silently to God. Then leave the candles burning throughout your devotional time or even longer. As you pass by the place throughout the day and see the candles burning, allow their light to remind you that your prayers are continually before God and that even now God is at work in your life and in the lives of those for whom you pray. You may also wish to reflect for a few moments on this prayer from the Gelasian Sacramentary:

> *O God of unchangeable power and eternal light, look favourably on thy whole Church, that wonderful and sacred mystery; and by the tranquil operation of thy perpetual providence carry out the work of [our] salvation; and let the whole world feel and see that things which were cast down are being raised up, and things which had grown old are being made new, and all things are returning to perfection through him from whom they took their origin, even Jesus Christ our Lord. Amen.*[25]

Scripture: Read Psalm 30.

Psalm 30 is one of the most powerful expressions of praise and thanksgiving in the psalter. The material of the psalm itself suggests that the speaker is praising God for deliverance from a serious illness or some other crisis that took him to death's very door. Expressions such as "You have healed me. . . . You brought up my soul from Sheol, restored me to life from among those gone down to the Pit," emphasize the relief at escape from death. Yet the title of the psalm, one of the few that indicates the psalm's use, calls it "A Song at the dedication of the temple" (Heb. house), and the Talmud locates its use in the dedication rites when the Jerusalem temple was purified after its desecration by Antiochus Epiphanes during the Maccabean war. Whether originally intended as a personal psalm of thanksgiving or for liturgical use, certainly an individual as well as a worshiping community may use it.

Learning the Music

Verses 1-5 simply express thanksgiving and praise for deliverance from a disaster. Again, the praise is directed totally toward God; there is no suggestion here that the speaker is in any way responsible for his own deliverance.

Reflect for a few moments on the phrase, *Weeping may linger for the night, but joy comes with the morning.* What is (or was) your night of weeping? What was (or would be) your morning of joy?

Verses 6-10 describe the speaker's attitudes and inner dispositions before the disaster and serve as the basis of his appeal to God for rescue. He describes his former naive *up* mentality, "As for me, I said in my prosperity, 'I shall never be moved.' By your favor, O Lord, you had established me as a strong mountain." When in your own life have you presumptuously felt that because things were going well for you, God must have been specially favoring you? When and how was your bubble of self-confidence pricked as was the speaker's when he says, "You hid your face; I was dismayed"? How did you feel when events overturned your naive confidence that God especially favored you?

In verses 8-9, the speaker makes a profound theological statement about the basis of human existence and the need for deliverance. The basis of his appeal for help is that if God does not rescue him, he will be unable to bear witness to God's faithfulness: "Will the dust praise you? Will it tell of your faithfulness?" He assumes that one purpose, if not *the* purpose, for human existence is the praise of God.

The Westminster Catechism says similarly that the chief end of human existence is to glorify God and enjoy God forever. In a real sense God's reputation for faithfulness is at stake in the speaker's crisis. He can recognize and publicly proclaim that reputation if God acts to deliver the speaker from the threat of death. How does this understanding of the basis for petition to God connect with your own experience? On what basis have you prayed for deliverance, and what was your primary concern—that God's faithfulness be seen or that your plight be remedied? What implications of this theology of petition might apply to your own prayer life?

Though the theology in the speaker's thinking is profound, it also is pre-Christian. Early Judaism had no doctrine of the afterlife. Death was the end of human existence. Period. One could not praise God if one died. How does Christian belief in the resurrection of Jesus from the dead illuminate and enlarge the theology of intercessory prayer in this psalm? Or, to put it another way, how does your Christian faith allow you to answer the question, "Will the dust praise you?"

"You have turned my mourning into dancing; you have taken off my sackcloth and clothed me with joy" is an exuberant expression of praise. Yet even here the psalmist keeps the purpose of deliverance firmly in view: "So that my soul may praise you and not be silent." Consider a time when you have experienced a sense of giddy relief and joy at being delivered from some crushing burden or danger. Did you reflect on the larger purpose or meaning that deliverance may hold for you, or did you just count yourself lucky or blessed and go on as you had before? If you have not reflected on what larger purpose your deliverance may have held, do so now.

In closing, pray the psalm through again, letting its exuberance and joy spill over into your own soul.

Singing the Song

Think of someone you know who is in need of deliverance from a serious threat or oppressive circumstances. If it's someone with whom you have a close relationship, share your insights from this psalm and let that person know that you will faithfully intercede for him or her, praying for deliverance.

Day 23

Preparation

If the practice of lighting a candle as you pray for someone appealed to you, continue it today. Or use whatever method of centering your thoughts and intentions on God works best for you—a hymn, a repetitive prayer-phrase, a breath prayer using the name of Jesus, or simply silence. You may also wish to use this prayer by Jane Austen as your own:

> *Incline us, O God! to think humbly of ourselves, to be saved only in the examination of our own conduct, to consider our fellow-creatures with kindness, and to judge of all they say and do with the charity which we would desire from them ourselves.*[26]

Scripture: Read Psalm 40.

Psalm 40 is a complex and curious composition. It appears to be composed of two separate pieces of poetry: first a prayer of thanksgiving for deliverance from death (verses 1-10), followed immediately by a petition for deliverance from enemies (verses 11-17). The relationship between these two disparate pieces is further complicated by the fact that verses 13-17 appear in their entirety, though somewhat changed, as Psalm 70. In their present juxtaposition, the thanksgiving for past deliverance appears to be the basis of the appeal for future deliverance. The writer of the Epistle to the Hebrews (10:5) states that the words recorded in verses 6-8 were spoken by Jesus, giving the reason for his willingness to die a sacrificial death. The use of this psalm by early Christians as an interpretive key to understanding the death of Jesus has colored its use ever since.

Learning the Music

The very first sentence, "I waited patiently for the Lord; he inclined to me and heard my cry," immediately establishes a connection between the quality of the experience of waiting and the experience of deliverance. In the speaker's mind, the link between patient waiting and deliverance is clear. Using your own *during* experiences as a guide, how would you describe the difference between patient and impatient waiting?

What does it mean to you to wait patiently for the Lord? Is such patient waiting a passive state or does it involve action?

If there is a causal link in the speaker's mind between patience and deliverance, there appears to be a similar link between deliverance and praise. Not only has God set my feet upon a rock, but God has also put a new song in my mouth, a song of praise to our God. This new song has an evangelical purpose: The psalmist sings the song so that many will see and fear and put their trust in the Lord. In the speaker's religious tradition, the natural response to an experience of deliverance would have been to make a sacrifice of thanksgiving in the temple. However, the speaker feels so strongly tuned-in ("you have given me an open ear") to God's purposes that he needs no ritual. He immediately proclaims the saving help of God to the whole worshiping community. What does this statement suggest to you about God's purposes in delivering us from the dark and deep pits in which we sometimes find ourselves? Reflect again on your own experiences of deliverance. Where in your own life do you see this linking of patience, deliverance, and praise? Did deliverance move you to praise? Was the praise, even if directed to God, a private sigh of relief that your long ordeal was over, or was it the occasion of helping others by bearing witness to God's faithfulness? How did you offer such a witness?

The speaker contrasts those who make the Lord their trust with those who go astray after false gods. This psalm sets this contrast between faith in the true God and faith in idolatry in the context of waiting for deliverance from some threatening or oppressive situation. In the speaker's day, this going astray "after false gods" might have meant offering sacrifices in pagan temples. What might it mean in our day? What false gods tempt us with offers of deliverance from our troubles? Where in your life do you witness the struggle between faith in God and faith in idols?

Despite the deliverance he has experienced already, the speaker appears to need more deliverance—this time from enemies who are gloating over his predicament. Yet he affirms his continued trust in the Lord as his deliverer and pleads that God will not delay in bringing fresh experiences of deliverance. On what does the speaker's confidence rest? From your own experience, explore the connection between memory of God's past help and your ability to wait patiently for God's help in the present. How might giving public testimony to God's help in times past strengthen you for a present ordeal?

In closing, pray the psalm aloud, trying to pray it with the tone of voice and emphasis implied in the words. Let your prayer encompass praise, relief, affirmation, petition, and trust just as the psalmist does.

Singing the Song

Consider ways your public witness to God's saving help and faithfulness could make a difference to someone struggling through a dark night. Explore opportunities that will enable you to be authentic and true to your own personality and, at the same time, unambiguously recognize that it was God who helped you.

Day 24

Preparation

From ancient times, not only in Christianity, many religious traditions have used incense as a symbol of human prayers rising to God. Tradition tells us that frankincense was one of the gifts of the Magi to the infant Jesus. The fragrance and the smoke of burning incense make their impact on our senses. When accompanied by a prayerful spirit, these sensations can communicate God's presence powerfully. If you have some incense and would like to burn a bit of it before beginning your prayer time, you may find this a useful way to draw your thoughts and inner impulses toward God. You may also want to use this prayer of a French philosopher of the seventeenth century to prepare yourself for prayer today.

O Lord, let me not henceforth desire health or life, except to spend them for you, with you, and in you. You alone know what is good for me; do, therefore, what seems to you best. Give to me, or take from me; conform my will to yours; and grant that, with humble and perfect submission, and in holy confidence, I may receive the orders of your eternal Providence; and may equally adore all that comes to me from you; through Jesus Christ our Lord. Amen.[27]

Scripture: Read Psalm 34.

In many respects, Psalm 34 is a companion to Psalm 25, which we studied last week. Psalm 34 is also an acrostic psalm (each poetic strophe begins with the succeeding letter of the Hebrew alphabet). Psalm 25 was an acrostic lament; this psalm is an acrostic song of praise for deliverance. The acrostic structure, while not evident in English translations, does not hold much appeal for modern, Western readers because it does not lend itself to thematic continuity. Yet both psalms evidence thematic movement. Psalm 34 begins with an ascription of praise; continues with a testimony to God's deliverance; and then moves into a wisdom mode, instructing others how to live in order to know God's blessings. It concludes with an affirmation of God as a God who delivers God's people.

Learning the Music

"I sought the Lord and he answered me, and delivered me from all my fears" is a straightforward testimony to God's faithfulness. The speaker does not attribute God's deliverance to his own deserving or goodness nor to mere good fortune but recognizes that his deliverance has originated in God's faithful love. His soul makes its boast in the Lord, and he describes himself as "this poor soul," emphasizing his own helplessness. In your own experience, where have you been aware of God's faithful love to you in the midst of your own helplessness?

The psalmist establishes a connection between fearing God (that is, recognizing God's transcendent otherness and holding God in reverential awe) and deliverance. He even goes so far as to say that "those who fear him have no want. . . those who seek the Lord lack no good thing." What is his evidence for that affirmation? Is it self-evident? What can you offer in support of such a statement?

In the wisdom section of the psalm, which begins with verse 11, the speaker affirms that the Lord is against evildoers but listens to the prayers of the righteous and "rescues them from all their troubles. The Lord is near to the brokenhearted, and saves the crushed in spirit." Notice that the speaker does not say that the righteous have no troubles from which they need deliverance. In other words, he is not arguing that righteous living earns the reward of prosperity or unalloyed comfort. In fact, the righteous need deliverance as much as anyone else: "Many are the afflictions of the righteous." In the speaker's eyes, the distinction between the righteous and the wicked is that the righteous experience deliverance from their afflictions while the wicked do not. Based on your experience, could you make the same affirmation? Why or why not? How valid is such an affirmation? How can you test its validity?

Close your time today by praying verses 4-10 again, this time thinking of the ways those statements have proved themselves in your own experience.

Singing the Song

Where, in your own life or in the life of someone close to you, would the exhortation "O taste and see that the Lord is good" be appropriately applied? If it is particularly appropriate for your own life at this moment, try to discover how you could heed it. If it is an exhortation especially appropriate for someone close to you, try to discover how you could communicate its truth to him or her.

Day 25

Preparation

Using a candle or incense or whatever method suits you best, withdraw inwardly from the distractions of the day ahead or the day just past. You may want to use this prayer of Lady Lucy Herbert to help you focus your inner thoughts for your prayer time:

> *Nothing has been capable, dear Lord, to hinder you from being all mine, neither heaven, nor your divinity, nor the gibbet of the cross: grant me the grace, that nothing may hinder me from being all yours, to whom I owe myself both for creation and redemption.*
>
> *'Twas never heard that in your mortal life, you lodg'd with any, which you did not liberally reward with your gifts: I beg you will do the same to your present habitation, which is my heart: let the touch of yours, which consecrates all things, sanctify my heart that it may be grateful to you.*[28]

Scripture: Read Psalm 65.

From beginning to end, Psalm 65 is a song of thanksgiving and praise, specifically related to the experience of deliverance. In verses 1-4, the psalmist praises God for deliverance through forgiveness of sins. The second movement, verses 5-8, praises God as the cosmic ruler whose awesome deeds of deliverance on behalf of Israel (an allusion to the Exodus) is the ground of hope for all people. Why this should be so is not made clear; it is simply affirmed. The implied connection is that weak and enslaved Israel could not have delivered itself from its Egyptian overlords; only God could do that. Finally the psalmist praises God for the abundant way God causes the earth to bear fruit so that people may enjoy its bounty.

Learning the Music

The setting of the first part of the psalm is public worship in the Temple. In traditional Jewish religion, the making of vows demonstrated the seriousness of one's petitions to God, as well as expressing faith in the answering of the petitions. So the psalmist addresses God as "O you who answer prayer!" In this case, the deliverance experienced is the deliverance from the effects of Israel's transgressions.

Since God answers prayer and forgives sin, deliverance takes the form of being rescued from those sins and brought near to God's presence in the Temple. The psalm makes a strong connection between forgiveness of sin and the perception of nearness to God. Sin alienates; forgiveness restores relationship. When have your own sins or transgressions made you feel far from God? When have you experienced the sense of restoration in relationship with God? To what extent was forgiveness involved in that sense of restoration and through whom or what was that forgiveness mediated?

The speaker links being chosen by God and brought near (restored to fellowship) to God with being connected to the worshiping community. What connection do you see between being brought near to God through forgiveness and being brought near to others with whom you share the experience of forgiveness? In other words, what is the relationship between deliverance and community? Explore these questions from the perspective of your own experience.

The second movement of the psalm celebrates God's deliverance of God's people through awesome deeds of creation and redemption. The speaker affirms that God is the hope of "all the ends of the earth." How do experiences of deliverance lead to hope? Think about this on the national level as well as on the personal level. How has an experience of deliverance strengthened your hope? How has an act of deliverance strengthened the hope of your nation or your people?

The psalm closes with praise of God because the earth is a bountiful producer of good things; the earth itself shouts and sings for joy. Explore the connections between the personal experience of deliverance and the perception that the creation itself is restored and renewed. How are personal deliverance and social deliverance related?

Close your time by praying this psalm aloud. Let it express for you personally the joy that accompanies deliverance from sin and from all that binds you and keeps you from experiencing God's abundance.

Singing the Song

Look around you and begin noting all the ways in which individuals, communities, and the earth itself stand in need of deliverance. Then begin to reflect on how your experience of deliverance could spill over into these other areas. Try to be as specific as possible in identifying what deliverance would mean in each instance. Then try to identify where your own individual experience could have an impact on the larger community or on the earth itself.

Group Session

Gathering

Numerous hymn settings of the psalms from this week's exercises may be found in hymnals of several denominations. Multiple settings of the same psalm offer an opportunity to observe and discuss the different interpretations of the psalm that the various musical settings convey. You may want to experiment with chanting one of the psalms using a psalm tone. Many of the major hymnals have such psalm tones, which are usually very ancient, either in the body of the hymnal itself or in a separate section near the front or back. Though chanting the psalms is an ancient practice, it is still very much alive in some denominational traditions.

Discussion

1. How did the expressions of praise for deliverance in the psalms for this week ring true or strike a discordant note with your own experiences?

2. The exercise for Day 21 asked you to explore the links between memories of God's past faithfulness and the ability to trust God in the present. How important are our memories in shaping our present sense of who we are and who God is? What powerful memories from your past have shaped your present understanding of your relationship to God?

3. Psalm 30 takes the form of a deeply personal expression of praise for deliverance, yet its designated use is a liturgical setting. What is the relationship between private prayer and corporate prayer? How do you understand your own prayer life to be connected to the prayer of the whole church?

4. If you did not read Hebrews 10:1-10 in your study of Psalm 40, you may want to read it aloud in the group setting. How do you react to this appropriation of Psalm 40 by a Christian author late in the first century to interpret the meaning of the death of Jesus?

5. The affirmation in Psalm 34 that the righteous experience God's deliverance while the wicked do not is a bold claim. What are the warrants for that claim? How can we verify such a statement? Is it a claim that any person, regardless of faith or lack of faith, could make?

6. John Wesley used the term *saved* to denote the whole experience of becoming rightly related to God through repentance and forgiveness. He affirmed that all people need to be saved, all people can be saved, and all people can know they are saved. What is your response to Wesley's thought? How do we know that God has forgiven us and that we are in right relationship with God? How is God's forgiveness mediated to us so that we know it both intellectually and experientially?

7. How do you view the connection between personal deliverance and the deliverance of all creation? Is deliverance (or *salvation* to use a related biblical term) primarily a personal spiritual phenomenon or a social phenomenon?

Closing

If time permits, close the session by praying Psalm 65 aloud together.

UPON

Psalms of Confidence and Trust

on *prep.* **1.a.** Used to indicate position above and supported by or in contact with. **b.** Used to indicate contact with or extent over (a surface) regardless of position. **d.** Used to indicate proximity. **f.** Used to indicate figurative or abstract position. **4d.** Used to indicate the object of perception or thought. **7.** Used to indicate a source or basis. **9.** Used to indicate belonging to.

—on *adv.* **1.** In or into a position or condition of being supported by or in contact with something. **2.** In or into a position of being attached to or covering something.

—on *adj.* **3.** Slang. Functioning or performing at a high degree of competence or energy.

up·on *prep.* On.

> He drew me up from the desolate pit,
>> out of the miry bog,
> and set my feet upon a rock,
>> making my steps secure.
>
> —Psalm 40:2

OUR JOURNEY HAS COME FULL CIRCLE. We are back *up* again. The plunge *down*; the painful struggles of *through*; the sometimes frustrating, sometimes restful state of *during*; and the soaring exhilaration of *from* lie behind us. We are *up*. Life is good again. Yet *up* is a different place than we remember it. This *up* has a solidity, a stability that was missing from our beginning point. The tiny word that signals that stability and solidity is *on*, which is attached to the *up*. We are not up in the air, we are not high as a kite, our head is not in the clouds. Instead we have both feet on the ground. As the writer of Hebrews put it, we have "a sure and steadfast anchor of the soul" (Hebrews 6:19). We are *upon*.

For many people this part of the journey does not occur until midlife, though it is by no means limited by age. However the maturity of *upon*, while possibly occurring in the young, more often gives witness to a certain quantity and quality of life experience. Younger people who have had few conflicts of identity and few vocational struggles may discover within themselves a confidence of faith and maturity of trust that comes later to the majority of Christians. Older people who have come late to an awareness of their inner journey with God or who have known great inner turmoil and unresolved conflicts from their younger days may not experience this confidence until much later. However most people experience a correlation between the events of midlife and the sense of security and confidence of the part of the journey that I call *upon*. The two things—life-experience and spiritual maturity are unrelated causally; they are simply correlative in many, if not most, cases.

People who are *upon* are people who know that life is not exclusively comprised of *up* experiences. They have had many disturbing encounters with the "changes and chances of this fleeting world," as the old collect puts it. They have learned that life is not a single melody in the treble clef. There are complex harmonies, dissonant chords, minor keys, and changes of rhythm that go into making up life's chorale. And they have learned how to sing the grace notes of that more profound composition. Even more, they have learned to know and trust the conductor. They have no illusions that the song will remain in a major key or attain a harmonic simplicity for long. They have already sung through some of the song, and they trust that the conductor has the remainder of the performance under control. Those who are *upon* continue to sing the songs of Zion, even when they must sing them in an alien land.

The psalms for this last week of the study express that mature confidence and trust in the conductor's skill, even though the song has not yet ended. We hear praises and expressions of thanksgiving similar in some respects to those psalms that began this journey but with significant differences. The lyrics may be the same; the performance of them is not.

We hear subtleties in the music we didn't hear before. Humility now colors the high notes of praise; wisdom tempers the low notes of depression and doubt. The command of the score is more competent and surefooted. Confidence born of experience pervades the whole. We may not know where the conductor will take us, but we are certain that the conductor will get us to the end of the piece and that the ending will be glorious. And so we sing out the praises of the One who sings in us, the One who is Composer and Conductor and Singer; who chooses our voices, our lips, our hearts "to sound God's praise in endless morn of light."[29]

Day 26

Preparation

Use this prayer of Erasmus of Rotterdam to prepare your own spirit for prayer. Erasmus was, perhaps, the most influential church scholar of his age; one whose writings prepared the way for the Protestant Reformation, though he himself never joined the Protestants.

> *O you, who are the true Sun of the world, ever rising and never going down; who, by your most wholesome appearing and sight, nourishes and gladdens all things, in heaven and earth; we implore you mercifully to shine into our hearts, that the night and darkness of sin, and the mists of error on every side, being driven away by the brightness of your shining within our hearts, we may all our life walk without stumbling, as in the day-time, and being pure and clean from the works of darkness, may abound in all good works which you have prepared for us to walk in. Amen.*[30]

Scripture: Read Psalm 66.

The psalm has two parts: The first (verses 1-12) is a call for the whole earth to praise God for the awesome deeds by which God delivered his people Israel from slavery in Egypt and for God's preservation, care, and saving faithfulness during times of severe testing. The language used to describe this testing is reminiscent of the language used by Isaiah, Jeremiah, and other prophets in describing the Exile, so probably the psalmist has the Exile and the return in mind. The second part of the psalm takes the form of a personal witness to God's steadfast love and faithfulness. The speaker vows to make certain offerings out of gratitude. He exhorts all those who fear God to learn from his example that God can be trusted and that God listens to the prayers of the righteous. Both parts of the psalm are part of congregational worship. The worshiping community celebrates God's deeds on behalf of all, while offering personal witness to those deeds.

Learning the Music

Some churches have a tradition of giving testimony or witnessing. Individuals stand and give a verbal description of something God has done for them that demonstrates, at least to them, that God is reliable and trustworthy. The purpose of testimony meetings was, and is where they still persist, mutual encouragement to trust God to bring one through the trials of life. If you were asked to give your testimony or your witness, what would you say? In what events in your life would you identify God's saving love at work to deliver you? What was your Exodus? What was your Exile and return? How did you experience God's help?

What is the value of public testimony, which implies the presence of a community, as opposed to a simple, personal prayer of thanksgiving? What is the place of community in identifying the awesome deeds of the Lord? Why do we sometimes prefer to keep our religion private?

The speaker in the individual testimony says that when he was in trouble, he vowed to offer certain sacrifices if God would deliver him. Now he is ready to make good on his part of the bargain—not as a way to gain God's favor but rather to express gratitude for favor already shown and experienced. These offerings, which are generous to the point of being lavish, are a concrete way of expressing gratitude. Most of us have probably bargained with God when we were in trouble: "God, if you'll just get me out of this, I'll . . ." If you ever made such a bargain, what did you promise? How have you kept that promise? Expressing gratitude concretely has value. What might be a concrete way for you to say thank you to God for helping you in your trouble?

Singing the Song

Part of the process of maturing spiritually is learning to bear witness to those experiences where we believe God has helped us. Rather than badgering someone to become a Christian or trying to convince someone of the intellectual superiority of Christian answers to life's questions, witnessing means giving testimony. It means telling what God has done for us and praising God's faithfulness before others. Try to identify a way in which you might give testimony to God's saving help to someone else; if not before your faith community, then to a friend or family member.

Preparation

Come to your time of prayer and meditation with the joyful expectation that God is here to meet with you. You may want to sing a favorite hymn or simply sit in silence while you compose yourself inwardly for this encounter with your divine partner. This collect from *The Book of Common Prayer* may help your preparation:

> *Almighty God, the fountain of all wisdom, you know our necessities before we ask and our ignorance in asking: Have compassion on our weakness, and mercifully give us those things which for our unworthiness we dare not, and for our blindness we cannot ask; through the worthiness of your Son Jesus Christ our Lord, who lives and reigns with you and the Holy Spirit, one God, now and forever. Amen.*[31]

Scripture: Read Psalm 84.

This is one of the most joyous psalms in the Bible. It expresses a longing for the courts of the Lord, that is, for the Temple on Mount Zion where God's presence symbolically dwelled. The speaker's longing, coupled with the mention of the highways to Zion (verse 5) and going through the valley of Baca (verse 6), evoke the image of pilgrims journeying toward Jerusalem for a festival of worship in the Temple. Because of the prayer request in verses 8-9 that God recognize the king ("our shield, . . . your anointed"), the Israelites probably used this psalm as part of royal processions to the Temple, where the people acknowledged and celebrated God's greater sovereignty. The earthly king receives recognition because he acknowledges that "the Lord God is a sun and shield" who bestows favor and honor.

Learning the Music

Even though we know that God's presence is everywhere, we still associate that presence with particular places or settings. God may be infinite and eternal, but we encounter God in the daily routines of our space- and time-bound existence. Those places of encounter with God become holy places for us. Someone has suggested that people often tend to sit in the same pew in church because that particular pew was the location of some memorable experience of God's presence. If you think back to the most significant experiences of your life when you felt that God was present to you, where would the courts of the Lord be for you—your local church? someone's living room? your college dorm? Perhaps it's not a place so much as an event or setting. When you feel a longing for a fresh encounter with God, to what do you attach that longing?

This psalm contains three beatitudes—statements that begin with "Happy are those . . ." or "Blessed are those . . ." In verse 4, it is "those who live in your house." In verse 5, it is "those whose strength is in you. . . . As they go through the valley of Baca" (a parched wilderness area). In verse 12, it is "everyone who trusts in you." Dwelling in God's house where God is praised continually; courage to journey to God's house, the place of God's presence; and trust in God's goodness are elements that make a person's life blessed or happy. Which of these elements are part of your own faith experience? Which are lacking? If one or more is lacking, how could it become part of your life?

This psalm defines the praise of God in the context of pilgrimage, a journey toward the holy or sacred, in which we recognize the presence of God and acknowledge God as the source of our life. Where are the highways to Zion for you? Where do you go to encounter God? Where are the valleys of Baca, the parched deserts of the soul through which you have to travel on your way to Zion? Do the highways to Zion and the valleys of Baca ever run together? In other words, where in your pilgrimage have you experienced God's abiding presence, even in the midst of times of spiritual dryness or doubt? How do you distinguish one highway from the other?

The psalm states that "those whose strength is in you [the Lord]" can turn the barren wilderness of Baca into a place of springs. Where in your own experience with God do you see a relationship between dependence upon God and the ability to transform deserts into fertile oases?

Verses 10-11 suggest a connection between praise and ethics. Being in God's house, even as a lowly doorkeeper is set over against living in the tents of wickedness. If the praise of God in this psalm is not just words of praise spoken in church, but a life lived in joyful and grateful acknowledgment of God as the source of life and all good, the connection between praise and ethics (behavior) becomes clearer. If one's behavior testifies to a dependence upon self (that is, self-made, self-sufficient, self-interest) rather than upon God, one cannot praise God—only oneself. Where do you see the connection between praise and ethics in your own life? Where is that connection weak or nonexistent? How do your ethical decisions and behavior testify to what you ultimately depend upon for your life? You may want to keep track of your decisions and actions for a period of time, perhaps using a journal to help you. Consider categorizing them as either belonging to the courts of the Lord or to the tents of wickedness. In this way you may look at your own life in a clearer light and discover those areas where you do not yet know the happiness of trusting in God.

Close your time today by praying Psalm 84 aloud.

Singing the Song

Do the categories "courts of the Lord" and "tents of wickedness" offer you any insights or clarity into the dynamics of your work environment, your church, or even the larger issues that face our society? These two categories could prove to be overly simplistic or extremely illuminating. Try analyzing your world (those relationships, activities, and environments in which you personally participate) using these two categories. Try to discover what changes, possibilities, or solutions such a perspective might offer.

Day 28

Preparation

Find your quiet place and quiet time. Spend a few moments repeating the Jesus Prayer (*Lord, Jesus Christ, Son of God, have mercy upon me*) until you feel an inner calmness and freedom from distractions of the day. Then meditate for a few moments on this prayer attributed to Saint Augustine of Hippo:

> *God of life, there are days when the burdens we carry are heavy on our shoulders and weigh us down, when the road seems dreary and endless, the skies gray and threatening, when our lives have no music in them, and our hearts are lonely, and our souls have lost their courage. Flood the path with light, turn our eyes to where the skies are full of promise; tune our hearts to brave music; give us the sense of comradeship with heroes and saints of every age; and so quicken our spirits that we may be able to encourage the souls of all who journey with us on the road of life, to your honor and glory. Amen.*[32]

Scripture: Read Psalm 91.

This psalm, one of the most beloved of all the psalms, has a long history of interpretation and devotion. Athanasius of Alexandria (A.D. 296–373) commended this psalm as one that could free a person from fears. Both Matthew and Luke (Matthew 4:5-7; Luke 4:10-11) place the words of verses 11-12 on the tempter's lips in their recounting of Jesus' temptation. The contrasting interpretations given these verses spoken by the tempter are the subject of many commentaries throughout church history.

One can discern the psalm's structure easily. The psalmist addresses verses 1-13 to "you who live in the shelter of the Most High." This "you" declares the Lord to be a refuge and a fortress. The second section (verses 14-16) is a divine affirmation of what was spoken in the first section. God says, in effect, "That's right. I will deliver and preserve those who trust in me."

Learning the Music

What does it mean to dwell in the shelter of the Most High? or to declare that God is our refuge and fortress?

We know what those words mean, but what does making God one's refuge really look like? How does one do it? What concrete actions does one take?

Think of an experience in your life when you took refuge in God or made God your fortress. What happened? How was God a refuge for you? What came of it?

Verses 9-10 have vast implications: "Because you have made the Lord your refuge, . . . no evil shall befall you, no scourge come near your tent." What is the truth of this statement in your own experience? How do you interpret these verses for other persons and communities? What definition of evil could make sense in this statement?

In the Gospel stories of Jesus' temptation, the tempter quotes verses 11-12 to Jesus as an inducement to launch himself from the pinnacle of the Temple to prove whether he really believes God has the power to preserve and protect him. Jesus responds that to do so would only prove that he was driven by self-aggrandizing and self-interested motives; such action would not really fulfill the promise of divine protection or prove anything about God's faithfulness. Where in your own life can you identify a situation that poses such a dilemma? On the one hand, trust in God's power and faithful love demands that you take some risks; on the other, your motives in taking the risks and the goal you seek are called into question. How does this psalm speak to that situation(s)? Where is the path of faithful obedience and trust that avoids the pitfall of presumption and manipulation?

The last statement, spoken by God, "With long life I will satisfy them, and show them my salvation," suggests that whatever else salvation may be, it includes some visible, concrete effects in this life. What would it mean for you to see God's salvation? From what do you need to be (or have you been) saved? Don't be overly vague or spiritual in answering this question; that is, God has saved or rescued me from my sins. Be specific. What sins? What does the rescue look like? How is your life different since the rescue?

Close your time by praying the psalm aloud, letting its promises and affirmations give buoyancy to your spirit.

Singing the Song

Who among your circle of family or friends or colleagues really needs to know that God is a refuge and a fortress? Who needs to see God's salvation? What can you do to help them experience the saving faithfulness of God?

Day 29

Preparation

Open your time today by meditating on this prayer of the late first-century bishop, Saint Clement of Rome:

For thou didst make manifest the everlasting constitution of the world through the forces set in operation. Thou, Lord, didst create the world. Thou who art faithful in all generations, righteous in judgments, marvelous in strength and excellence, wise in creating and prudent in establishing all that was made, good in what is seen and kindly among them that trust in thee, merciful and pitiful—forgive our sins and unrighteousnesses, our trespasses and failings. Reckon not every sin of thy servants and handmaidens, but cleanse us with the cleansing of thy truth, and make our steps straight that we may walk in holiness and righteousness and simplicity of heart, and may do what things are good and well pleasing before thee and our governors. Yea, Lord, let thy face shine upon us for good in peace, that we may be sheltered by thy strong hand and delivered from all sin by thine uplifted arm. . . .

O thou who alone art able to do with us these good things and others more abundant, thee we praise through the high priest and protector of our souls, Jesus Christ, through whom be glory and majesty to thee both now and for all generations and for ever and ever. Amen.[33]

Scripture: Read Psalm 103.

Psalm 103 is one of the most profound affirmations of God's nature and grace in the whole Bible. The carefully structured psalm artistically presents a comprehensive catalogue of God's praiseworthy characteristics. It begins and ends with the exhortation to "Bless the Lord," and everything in between is an elaboration or rationale for the exhortation. It is also composed (in Hebrew) of twenty-two poetic lines, corresponding to the twenty-two letters of the Hebrew alphabet—another A–Z hymn of praise. The chief characteristic of God's nature, revealed in all God's dealings with his people, is steadfast love (Heb. *hesed*). The reference to steadfast love is repeated five times in the psalm, three times paired with compassion or mercy (Heb. *rhm*). This steadfast love and compassion is directed principally to the forgiveness of *iniquity*, *transgressions*, and *sin*—all the words for human wrongdoing and error used in the Hebrew Scriptures. God directs this primary activity toward all "those who fear him" (repeated three times). This fear is the reverence for God that is expressed through obedience to God's commandments and trust in God's forgiveness.

Learning the Music

A rabbi once said, "When you Christians pray before eating, you ask God to bless the food; when we Jews pray before eating, we bless God for giving us the food." Psalm 103 begins and ends by blessing God. To bless means to sanctify by some religious rite or to honor. God's name, which stands for God's whole character and being, is honored or made holy by the public rite of remembering and reciting God's deeds on behalf of God's people.

Notice the parallel structures of the psalmist's opening blessing. He blesses the Lord who forgives, who heals, who redeems, who crowns, who satisfies. If you were to bless the Lord, what would you remember and recite? Which of the psalmist's affirmations about the activity of God could you personally affirm?

Many people have grown up in religious circles that exercised guilt as a means of control and manipulation. Such guilt-based spirituality often casts God in the role of the judge, keeping strict account of human misdoings and punishing those who do wrong. Such religion commonly leads either to a misguided perfectionism or rebellious libertinism. How does this psalm's picture of God differ from the spirituality of guilt? In your life, how has guilt been part of your understanding of and relationship to God? Is the God whom you personally experience one who "does not deal with us according to our sins, nor repay us according to our iniquities, . . . as far as the east is from the west, so far [God] removes our transgressions from us" or is your God the judge who is making a list and checking it twice in order to find out who's naughty and nice? (You might explore the connections between your emotional image of God and the popular conception of Santa Claus.)

The thrice-repeated phrase "for those who fear him" qualifies somewhat the image of God as one who steadfastly shows mercy. This suggests that God's forgiving nature is not merely apathetic indulgence masquerading as kindness. The psalmist also affirms God as one who works vindication and justice for all who are oppressed. In other words, God is not indifferent to evil. Rather, God's nature as one who forgives and does not punish is a nature discovered by those who revere God, who regard God as the center for life's orientation and coherence. Forgiveness implies wrongdoing that is recognized and acknowledged as such. If we cannot do wrong against God because God simply overlooks or indulges us in whatever we do, then God has no reason to forgive us.

Yet this psalm's celebration of God's nature as a forgiving God makes it abundantly clear that both the psalmist and Israel know that they have done much that needs forgiveness. John Newton eloquently expressed that recognition in his well-known hymn "Amazing Grace": "Amazing grace! How sweet the sound that saved a wretch like me! I once was lost, but now am found; was blind, but now I see." Where in your own life have you discovered, or where do you need to discover, the close connection between your identity as a sinner and God's identity as the one who forgives your sins? What will it mean for you to fear God?

The psalm ends with an exhortation, not only to mortals but to all the heavenly hosts and all creation, to join the psalmist in blessing God. Do you ever think of your own life and relationship to God in such cosmic terms? How are the exhortations, "Bless the Lord all his hosts. . . . Bless the Lord, all his works" and "Bless the Lord, O my soul" related in your own understanding? How would such a relationship find concrete expression in your life?

Close your time by praying the psalm aloud. Let its poetry and music sing its message into your heart.

Singing the Song

In your circle of family and friends, try to observe images of God as angry judge rather than forgiving parent at work in what others say and do. Try to discern how you could be a witness to a God, whose first and best name—in Charles Wesley's words—is Love.

Day 30

Preparation

To prepare yourself for praying the most beloved psalm of all, reflect for a few moments on this prayer from Saint Augustine's *Confessions*:

> *O good omnipotent, who so cares for every one of us, as if you cared for each alone; and so for all, as if all were but one! Blessed are the ones who love you, and their friends in you, and their enemies for you. I behold how some things pass away that others may replace them, but you never depart. O God, my Father, supremely good, Beauty of all things beautiful, to you will I entrust whatever I have received from you, and so shall I lose nothing. You have made me for yourself, and my heart is restless until it rests in you.* [34]

Scripture: Read Psalm 23.

Perhaps no passage of scripture, other than the Lord's Prayer, has had so lasting and profound an impact upon the spirituality of millions. That impact is due in no small part to the power of the controlling metaphor: God as Shepherd of God's people. In Christian usage, the author of the Gospel of John has appropriated that metaphor and applied it to Jesus in the powerful "I am the good shepherd" passage, thereby firmly grounding Christian thinking about Jesus as the incarnation of a caring God. There are other reasons for our understanding of God as one who cares. The personal pronoun "my" in the first line makes this psalm a deeply personal and individual expression of trust in God's providential care. Also this psalm—unlike so many of the others—asks nothing of God; it is a pure and simple affirmation of trust and confidence in God.

Psalm 23 frequently serves as a funeral text because of its calm and tranquil expression of confidence in God in the very face of our last, still-powerful, though ultimately defeated enemy: death. Until recently, the majority of Western Christians knew Psalm 23 by heart. Even as recently as a decade ago, most persons attending a funeral could join in the oral recitation of Psalm 23 from memory. Today fewer and fewer young people receive religious instruction and scripture memorization has fallen out of fashion in many churches. This most beloved of all psalms is no longer in the hearts and on the lips of the majority of God's people to offer them a powerful source of strength and comfort. The magnitude of that loss may be incalculable.

Learning the Music

The image the word *shepherd* conjured up in the minds of people of the ancient Near East was rich in connotations. The shepherd was the overseer, caretaker, nurse, nanny, disciplinarian, doctor, protector, provider, and more to the sheep. The shepherd was personally engaged with each aspect of the lives of the flock. So the affirmation "The Lord is my shepherd" is the same affirmation as the second half of that line: "I shall not want." To be the sheep of this shepherd is not to be in want of anything necessary for life and well-being. What does that affirmation mean to you personally? How have you experienced God's care as your shepherd? If this affirmation is not one that you can readily make, what other images of God can you affirm?

Being in the personal care of this shepherd does not remove the sheep from danger. The sheep must negotiate "the valley of the shadow of death" and face enemies whose presence is persistent and discomfiting. The sheep experiences security and well-being—not in the absence of evil or danger but in the midst of it. How is this possible? How have you known such security in the midst of danger in your own experience and relationship with God?

It is unlikely that any Israelite could have recited Psalm 23 without hearing echoes and allusions to the saving deeds of God in the Exodus, the giving of the Law at Sinai, the forty-year sojourn in the wilderness during which they wanted for nothing. Each individual recited his or her affirmation of God's shepherding care in the context of the community's experience of God's saving deeds in its collective history. So this psalm is not just an expression of how any individual "sheep" feels at any given moment. Rather, it is a confession that is at once public and historical; I confess God as my shepherd, not only because I have experienced God's care, but also because I belong to a community that has experienced God's shepherding care. This broader perspective delivers us from locating God's presence or absence entirely in our own individual experience. We receive a broader context in which to interpret the individual "ups" and "downs" of our life.

God's faithfulness to each individual sheep is intimately related to God's faithfulness to the whole flock, and that larger faithfulness enables me to understand and evaluate my own situation differently. How do you see this relationship between the individual experience of God's care and the history of God's care for the larger flock in the context of your own life? How might it offer you a new perspective on your own life?

The word *follow* in the phrase, "Surely goodness and mercy shall follow me all the days of my life" does not mean "to come after or behind"; rather it means "to come from behind and overtake." In the midst of our lives, in the midst of danger, in the presence of enemies, God's goodness and mercy overtakes us and surrounds us. Describe a time in your life when you were conscious of being overtaken by God's care for you. How did that overtaking occur? Through what or whom did that overtaking come?

Close this time by praying the Shepherd Psalm aloud, affirming God's tender and persistent care for you.

Singing the Song

If you have not committed Psalm 23 to memory, begin to do so. What we know by heart tells us who we are and whose we are. God's care for us most often comes through other people. Begin to look for ways in which you may be led to be the defending rod, rescuing staff, or the healing anointing oil in the life of someone who needs to experience God's shepherding care.

Group Session

Gathering

If you or someone in the group has a recording of Johannes Brahms's setting of "How Lovely Are Thy Dwellings," you may want to play it to begin the session to see how Psalm 84 has inspired great composers. The musical *Godspell* has a lively setting of Psalm 103: "O Bless the Lord, My Soul." Almost all hymnals have multiple hymn-settings of Psalm 23. Three of the most familiar and common are "The Lord's My Shepherd, I'll Not Want"; "The King of Love My Shepherd Is"; or "My Shepherd Will Supply My Need." Sing one or more of these to see how the same psalm inspires hymnists differently.

Discussion

1. Spend some time discussing the characterization of *upon* and its differences or similarities to *up*. Are the differences valid ones or not? Why?

2. Give a few moments to reflecting on the study as a whole. If you were previously unfamiliar with the psalms, in what ways did this study help you? If you were already accustomed to using the psalms as a resource for prayer, how has the study helped you?

3. Which of this week's psalms was the most meaningful for you personally? Which was the most problematic for you? Why?

4. Psalm 66 states that God has been faithful in caring for his people through some severe tests, but God is also responsible for those severe tests which Israel faced: "For you, O God, have tested us; you have tried us as silver is tried. You brought us into the net; you laid burdens on our backs; you let people ride over our heads; we went through fire and through water; yet you have brought us out to a spacious place (Psalm 66:10-12). How do we reconcile that understanding of God's care with the image of God as the shepherd who "leads me beside still waters; [who] restores my soul"; whose rod and staff defend the flock against all enemies and who abundantly feeds the sheep?

5. What is the connection between one's individual experience of God as a caring God and one's relationship to a community that proclaims and worships a caring God?

6. The exercise on Psalm 103 raised the issue of the different emotional images of God that people have. For some, God is a God of judgment to be feared; for others, a God of forgiveness to be loved. What is the difference between our theology of God and our emotional image of God? Which is more likely to influence our behavior? How do we develop our emotional images of God?

7. How many in the group know Psalm 23 from memory? What value and comfort do persons derive from this memorization? What value might persons derive from knowing other portions of scripture by memory?

Closing

If you have not already done so, sing a setting of Psalm 23 together. If you have, read Psalm 103 aloud.

Notes

1. James Limburg, "Book of Psalms," *Anchor Bible Dictionary*, Volume 5 (New York: Doubleday, 1992), 523.

2. Athanasius, *Ad Marcellinum*, cited in James Luther Mays, *Psalms* (Louisville, KY: Westminster/John Knox Press, 1994), 1.

3. This and all subsequent word definitions that appear on the introductory page for each week are taken from the *New American Heritage Dictionary*, 3rd edition (New York: Houghton Mifflin Company, 1992).

4. *The Book of Common Prayer* (New York: Oxford University Press, 1990), 90–91.

5. *The Oxford Book of Prayer* (New York: Oxford University Press, 1986), 66.

6. *The Book of Common Prayer*, 100.

7. John Wesley, "A Collection of Prayers for Families," from *Works of Wesley*, vol. 11 (Grand Rapids, MI: Zondervan Publishing House, n.d.), 255.

8. *The Book of Common Prayer*, 112.

9. *The Oxford Book of Prayer*, 130–31.

10. Harry Emerson Fosdick, *The Meaning of Prayer* (New York: Association Press, 1916), 153.

11. *The Book of Common Prayer*, 461.

12. *The Meaning of Prayer*, 58.

13. *The Book of Common Prayer*, 229.

14. *The United Methodist Book of Worship* (Nashville, TN: United Methodist Publishing House, 1992), 528.

15. *The Book of Common Prayer*, 231.

16. *The Oxford Book of Prayer*, 133.

17. *Book of Common Worship* (Louisville, KY: Westminster/John Knox Press, 1994), 22.

18. *The Oxford Book of Prayer*, 107.

19. *Book of Common Worship*, 828.

20. *The Oxford Book of Prayer*, 81.

21. *The Meaning of Prayer*, 138.

22. *Book of Common Worship*, 829.

23. *Book of Common Worship*, 830–31.

24. *The Meaning of Prayer*, 8.

25. *The Oxford Book of Prayer*, 247.

26. *The Oxford Book of Prayer*, 164.

27. *The Meaning of Prayer*, 59.

28. *The Oxford Book of Prayer*, 160.

29. From George Frederick Handel's *Let Their Celestial Concerts All Unite*.

30. *The Meaning of Prayer*, 119.

31. *The Book of Common Prayer*, 231.

32. *Book of Common Worship*, 828.

33. F. Forrester Church and Terrence J. Mulry, eds., *The Macmillan Book of Earliest Christian Prayers* (New York: Macmillan, 1988), 18–19.

34. *The Meaning of Prayer*, 42.